Love We Live

Book Two - Treasures of my Sacred Path

Kye Crow

Arkheart Foundation

Love We Live

Published by Arkheart Foundation

First Published 2022 in a limited edition 'Whispers of the Camels'

Copyright text @Kye Crow

Cover art by catspyjamasdesign@gmail.com

Copyright cover image @catspyjamasdesign

All rights reserved. No part of this publication may be reproduced whole or in part, stored in a retrievable system, or transmitted in any form or by any means, electronic, mechanical, photocopying, recording, or otherwise, without permission of the copyright holder or publisher, other than for 'fair use' as brief quotations in articles and reviews.

Dedicated to my Gill

Even when we are face down in the dirt,

I love the way we laugh.

Everyday we turn the ordinary

into the extraordinary.

Love You so VERY MUCH

Honouring

I began writing this book while living in Barkindji country and it was finally completed on the banks of a river on sacred Yuwaalaraay country where we were blessed to know a beautiful elder who embodied such wisdom and love, we felt truly deeply welcomed. We love you Vic.

We pay our deepest respect to all the different tribes whose country we have travelled through.

We honour you all, past, present and future.

You are the ancient roots of the tree and without you, the tree falls over.

One

Whispers of the Camels

How innocently I made that phone call. Completely unaware that the consequences of that day would shift the direction of my life forever, and that what was about to enter my life would lead me so far away from my comfort zones that I would never walk the well-worn paths again.

I had tossed and turned all through the night after our conversation. Dreaming up one excuse after another to bail out, but deep down I knew I wouldn't use any of them. I had offered to help and I felt honour bound to go.

Now there were several reasons I was not looking forward to the day. In truth, even though I had made a friendly offer to help someone who'd just split up from her partner, I barely knew Adi. I liked her, was curious about her, but often found her very distant to be around. The prospect of spending an entire day with her felt a little daunting.

But there was a much more pressing reason and one I had not anticipated when I made my innocent offer. You see I had imagined baby-sitting her daughter, helping her move some boxes of stuff, even cooking her a dinner after a long day - but instead she had roped me into moving two camels, twenty kilometres. She had leapt on my offer of help with such unexpected eagerness for someone usually so restrained, I couldn't find any way to back out. I knew I wouldn't be any help to her. I had only met a camel once before and he had been drooling copious amount of saliva and had lunged at me with such aggression, I had no desire to *ever* meet one again.

Yes, I felt scared! I wanted to run away as fast as I could but the day had an inevitability about it that was stronger than me. It was happening whether I liked it or not.

Adi arrived just after dawn with a friend I'd not met before and I wasn't immediately enamoured. On first meeting he seemed a bit full of himself. In his early forties, wearing high heeled cowboy boots and perfecting a cocky strut, Adi introduced me to Eagle. While his overall attire was cowboy, black shirt tucked into neat and tidy jeans, there was also an aspect of hippy. Hanging around his neck was a large quartz crystal amulet and his black Akubra hat was adorned with feathers.

In his hand he carried a jumbo pack of cigarettes, prepared and ready to chain smoke anywhere. I had no idea then that by the end of the day I would be shaking like a leaf and sucking on Winnie blues with him.

He was loud and boisterous and slapped me on the back as if I was a long lost friend and as the three of us piled into Adi's car, I couldn't help noticing - Eagle was the only one enjoying himself.

For twenty kilometres we drove down a bumpy corrugated red dirt road, through a landscape of giant tumbleweeds and salt bush, laced with patches of wildflowers. The desert had grown lush from all the recent rains and I couldn't help feeling deeply moved by the splendour of the bush, the terracotta coloured road and the flocks of white corellas that would swoop across the bright blue sky, twisting and turning and swirling in the light.

By the time we pulled into the paddock where Adi's camels were, I had softened to the experience. I had let go of the fight, I was even warming to Eagle who wasn't as brash or full of himself as my first impressions had led me to believe. He was actually really likeable and had a rare childlike quality about him that led him to embrace life with excitement and even though he was a horse man with no experience of camels, he was pretty confident his equine skills would come in handy.

While Adi tooted the horn of her car to call the camels in, Eagle and I walked out to a small red sandhill, hoping to get high enough to see the camels coming in from a distance. The paddock was so big, you could walk for a day and not hit a fence - but the camels were familiar with the car horn and Adi was certain they would come.

Twenty minutes passed of horn tooting and searching for humps and finally we saw them weaving their way through the mulga and witchetty bush, to us. They walked in a haze, with the dust billowing around them and from my distance, the harsh desert light made them look as if they'd been bleached. All my fears were forgotten and I felt a flush of excitement. We sat for a while, watching as they approached and as they got closer Eagle and I began walking towards them, eager to meet them. Adi had reassured us they were all friendly.

I was standing innocently out on the flat as the first camel came towards me. He was so much bigger than I'd anticipated from a distance and he barged straight up to me, totally ignoring my outstretched hand. He had absolutely zero respect for my space and I found this frightening. He stood towering above me menacingly, with his body almost pressed up against mine and his drooling mouth smeared right up against my face.

I had not expected this and although I was doing my best not to panic, inside I was freaking out.

Deep breath Kye, don't panic, best not to run, deep breath, that's it my girl you're doing fine, just keep breathing and stay calm.

It was so hard. I was struggling not to panic and at the same time trying to look casually around me for a safe place to reach, but the car or the nearest tree was too far away and Adi seemed completely oblivious to my situation. There was nowhere close enough for me to go, and the camel was getting more and more menacing, jumping around me and kicking out its legs. I couldn't even see a stick on the ground I could use to defend myself.

I felt so intimidated, my mouth was dry with fear. I had no idea what to do, I only knew it was wise to stay calm. If I ran his game would be on. It was in that moment of desperate realisation that I had nowhere safe to go that I saw Eagle and it's a moment I shall never forget.

He was ambling towards me, totally absorbed in his thoughts. His well-worn black Akubra hat giving some shade from the sun, his face a picture of contentment, he looked as if he was in the midst of recalling happy memories. The time he had tamed the wild stallion, or lassoed the runaway cow, or swung through the trees like Tarzan. We had heard many tales of Eagle's daring feats on the drive down and as I watched him approach, I felt myself sigh. Eagle would know what to do. Eagle would help. Relief flooded through me.

There is something that happens when you're drenched with fear. Everything appears to slow down and there is a sharpening of senses. Every detail is noticed, every heart beat heard. I saw the exact moment that Eagle became present to his surroundings. I watched the contented smile slip away from his face. I saw him stop dead in his tracks as danger hit him in the guts. I felt the very moment my intimidator took all his attention from me and focused it on Eagle with such a ferocious intensity, he was almost licking his lips in anticipatory pleasure as he watched this lone cowboy approach. There was a brief moment when Eagle and the camel locked eyes and then Eagle, with no pretence of bravery, turned and took off running for his life, his high heeled cowboy boots kicking up the dust leaving hard edged tracks in the desert sand as the red maniac of a camel galloped after him.

I was so shaken by the experience I collapsed on the ground laughing hysterically. I had tears rolling down my face. I felt sick and wanted to have a shit all at the same time and I only began breathing again when I saw Eagle make it to safety!

Eagle and I from that moment on were united in our fear of camels. We clung to each other, initiated into our camel terror together. Forever brother and sister, bonded eternally by the day we had almost been trampled by the rogue red camel from hell. Neither of us were any help to Adi, who made no attempt to even conceal her scorn for us.

It had taken hours in the hot sun to catch one young camel because Adi was doing it single-handed. Every time the camel ran towards Eagle or me we would run as if we were being chased and hide, petrified in the trees.

Finally Adi, with the skill of a well-seasoned cowgirl which she wasn't, lassoed and caught the young camel she wanted to take. Kunkaa was only six months old and her mother was in such poor condition she looked like a walking skeleton. Separating Kunkaa from her mother was a hard choice for anyone to make, but If Adi didn't take the baby, mum would surely die.

I felt so relieved when the three camels were finally tethered from the back of Adi's small sedan car and we set off on the slow and bumpy drive home. It was getting late in the day and there was no doubt we would be driving well into the dark.

Adi's expectations of the jobs she thought I would be suitable for constantly kept falling outside of my 'can do' zone. Arming me with a huge block of wood, she wanted me to hang out the front passenger window and bash the big red camel who had terrorised me and Eagle with a block of wood in an attempt to stop him eating the car!

We had learned his name was Abdul and he was straining on his rope to get the rear vision mirror in his mouth. I gave him a wee whack, nothing happened. It made zero impact and did not deter him from his focus on the destruction of the mirror.

"Hit him harder," Adi said impatiently. Even though this camel had put me through hell, hitting him was not something I could do. We swapped places in a stony silence and I drove, at five kilometres an hour. I faced hours of driving in the heat with sweat pouring down my face and almost zero conversation with Adi, but at least driving was something I *could* do.

Way off in the distance, just a pinprick on the horizon, was Eagle. Despite the searing heat of the sun he had refused to ride in the car and had vowed never to go near a camel again, ever. Nothing we said would convince him to come anywhere near the car. He knew the camels were on short ropes, but he wasn't taking *any* chances.

He hobbled the twenty kilometres back in his high heeled cowboy boots, blistering his swollen feet and I would have joined him if I could have. I would have hobbled down that rough desert road and blistered my feet with him. It was cloying in the car. Adi does not suffer fools and is often so remote, and the silence that had settled between us was suffocating.

I was so relieved as we got closer to town to see Gill driving out to meet us. As the light had faded he had decided to come and see if we were all ok. My biggest concern was Eagle who had fallen so far behind, we had not seen him for a few hours. Gill drove back and found him, staggering along in the dark, badly dehydrated and bright red from sun burn.

The two male camels we'd towed behind had been revolting creatures. The other male camel was in season and bubbling froth and spittle all over the place. The only redemption for their species was little Kunkaa who despite leaving her mother behind, had walked the twenty kilometres stoic and uncomplaining. Regardless of the grace of this chocolate brown calf, I, just like Eagle, never wanted to see another camel EVER, EVER again.

It wasn't until a week later that I found out something that Adi had failed to tell us, or perhaps it was something she had failed to admit to herself, but Eagle and I were not the only ones who had been predated on by Abdul. While he behaved like an angel for Adi and her ten year old daughter, the list of people he had terrorised was lengthy and included experienced cameleers who had climbed trees to escape him, and police officers who had been chased around their squad car and eventually had to stay on the roof until help came. I even heard of one woman who had spent hours running between her car and her gate that she was trying to open so she could drive out to work. She didn't make it to work that day.

While it was a miracle no-one had ever been hurt, it was even more miraculous that Abdul, in his reign of terror, had not been shot.

Naughty Abdul had originally come from the small outback town of Oodnadatta, hand reared and allowed to grow up without clear boundaries. Drinking beer in the pub, he was generally seen as source of amusement until the cute antics of a baby camel became dangerous the bigger he got. It's pretty sad to imagine the confusion he must have felt when he got driven out of town but Abduls story is not unique. Numerous tales exist of people who have hand reared orphan camels, brought them up without any boundaries or discipline, allowing them to come into the house, laughing at all sorts of dysfunctional behaviour and then shooting them when they become too dangerous to be around.

But Abdul was one of the lucky ones and was rescued by Adi from his lone life on the local rubbish tip when she trekked through Oodnadatta with her own camels. She obviously adored him, but after the day I'd had with him, I had yet to understand why and I was certain I never would.

I was so relieved when I said goodbye to Adi and her camels. It had taken us fifteen hellish hours since leaving early that morning. I was dirty and tired and had not eaten all day. I just wanted to get home.

Eagle and I clung to each other as we said goodbye, tears rolling down our faces and promised to stay in touch, both still shaking from the traumas of the day, both adamant our camel days were done. I had told Gill as we drove home, "I am definitely NOT a camel woman Gill." I was so clear about that.

It had been a long time since I'd dreamt of Gill walking towards me leading three humped beasts and it would be another year before, like sunshine streaming through the clouds, that I'd finally make that connection. Camels were coming into my life whether I liked it OR NOT! And they had already begun.

I dreamt of them almost every night and the word camel popped up everywhere. I'd pass two old ladies chatting over trolleys at the supermarket, their conversation a muted blur, then radiant and clear the word camel would leap out. As I sat watching the weather report on TV, I was convinced that amid the raised dust and endless heat the word camel had been mentioned. When I sat quietly on our veranda at night I could hear the camels soft-bellied moans so similar to the call of the whales being carried in on the wind. It was happening for Gill too, subliminally camels had invaded our lives and neither of us could stop thinking about them!

When Adi offered us Kunkaa a few weeks later, I was unexpectedly delighted, although a little surprised. I thought Adi had given up on me completely and I felt honoured she'd entrust her little calf to us. Kunkaa means crow in Pitjantjatjara aboriginal language and even if I didn't yet have an affinity with the camel, I definitely had one with the crow. She arrived on the same day as Jianti, another young camel cow we bought for $300, just so that Kunkaa would have a friend.

How innocently I welcomed them. How easily they wooed me with their big dark eyes, long lashes and their charming and adorable ways. I didn't just fall in love - I dived in, naked and bare. When I was with the camels I knew I was exactly where I was meant to be, nothing else existed. The normal mundane stresses of life, bills and obligations faded into a past life. If I had known then what I'd have to let go off to keep them in my life, I don't know if I would have been brave enough to let them in. I might have kept the gate firmly closed, but it's often the most unexpected journeys that yield the greatest treasure.

I know that now, but I didn't then.

Two

The Soft Hum of the Desert

There's an old saying in Alice that drifts around the smoking campfires, as billies blacken and boil and mangy dogs dig hip holes to sleep in the desert sand. It's passed from one swagman to another as they rest in the shade of the giant gums that grow in the dry river bed and it goes

If you see the Todd river run three times, you'll never leave the Alice. You're as good as a local, and that's something that usually takes years!

The river had run twice in our first year in Alice but it wasn't until the third time it flowed that something special began to happen for us.

We had struggled to understand what had bought us to this tiny desert town in the middle of Australia. It had felt so right when we had left Cairns on a whim, driving over 2,000 kilometres with barely any cash and yet nothing really flowed when we arrived. We had spent the first year living in a tin shed - it was a huge open space and I loved so much about it, yet it baked us in summer and froze us in winter when everything turned to ice.

Even so, we'd made it a home. We hung colourful rainbow sheets from the walls, put in a giant pot-belly and covered the bare earth floors with carpets and I loved living on that soft earth floor. I planted huge tubs of daffodils that sat where the light fell through the doorless doorway. Gill made shuttered windows that we could open up to nature and close down when it rained. On one wall of the shed we set a window I'd hand painted, and emblazoned across the swirls of vivid colour was the word TRUST. We had created a home with the resonance of a temple, a creative and happy haven from the world, but living there was always a double-edged sword.

We woke up one morning to a venomous brown snake consuming a mouse right beside our bed. I preferred the snakes to stay outside, but they didn't bother me as much as surviving the elements did. There were times I would be shivering and so cold I couldn't even remember what it was to be warm. Focusing on my painted window kept me going. In every dark moment I was reminded to trust, but when the shed flooded it was the last damn straw!

We were on the verge of leaving Alice, well and truly over the shed and thinking *It's obviously not happening here for us*, when we saw the Todd river run for the third time.

We had stood on the dry riverbank listening to the peculiar sound that was filling the air and neither of us could place or explain what it was. It was as if the air was filled with static and its roar was getting louder and louder. And then it came. A grubby, frothy, muddy mess of raging water that had picked up every bit of rubbish in its dry bed, passing us in a torrent of old wine casks, plastic bags, and empty drink bottles.

Alice has a large Aboriginal population and with a no alcohol policy at the town camps, the dry river bed was often the place the revellers met to share a cask. I loved those early morning drives into town, past the Todd's numerous bush camps with smoke spiralling from their fires, people asleep under blankets and camp dogs stretched out in the sand. Often on the drive back home, their blankets would be hanging from the branches of the gum trees they camped under, drying out from the early morning dew. Old women would be bent over gathering wood to rekindle the dying fire, old and scruffy dogs would be sniffing around camp for scraps. When rain fell up north and the flow finally reached Alice, the revellers would return to their homes and the dry bed would get its much needed cleanse. I had only ever seen it flowing. I had never seen it begin to flow, but even with all its tide of rubbish, it was invigorating. I couldn't help remembering that old saying and it seemed so serendipitous when we bumped into a regular customer of our colourful clothes and she told us about a house that was coming up for rent which she was certain had our name written all over it.

"It's got huge big wide verandahs," she told us, having to shout to be heard over the rivers roar. "There's a spa bath, it's even got a pond inside the house. Are you interested?"

Am I interested? YES I BLOODY AM! And I could see when I looked at Gill, he was too!

I barely slept that night. I was so excited at the possibility of a home and I felt this unexpected relief that it looked as if we were going to stay. I hadn't realised until then that I didn't want to leave Alice. I loved living there. I just wanted out of the shed.

The house for rent was in the same street we lived on so early the next morning we went down to have a look. As we walked down the long treed driveway I could not believe my eyes. *Yes, yes, yes* I was singing to myself. *Finally, my God, it's happening!* We climbed the stairs of the verandah to knock on the door. There were huge terracotta pots full of lush plants, giant pots with water gardens, lilies and fish. It was so serene I was purring and as I knocked on the glass front door I could see a huge statue of a golden buddha sitting inside. I was holding my breath, praying this would happen. *Oh Puhleeeeese!* The guy who answered the door looked confused when we told him why we were there. There had been some far-flung whimsy of a thought to rent it out at some point over the next ten years, maybe. But that was it.

I was devastated!

As we walked back down the drive of this glorious home it took every ounce of strength for me to resist collapsing on the ground and sobbing. I felt so disappointed, though I was soon distracted. Just as we came out the gate our attention was drawn to the overgrown block directly opposite with a forlorn looking house sitting in the midst of waist high dead buffle grass. A faded FOR SALE sign hung lopsidedly on the locked gate. It was the complete and utter opposite of the beautiful home we had just glimpsed. There was nothing charismatic about it and any charm it may have had failed to reach us as we stood looking from the gate. I had no idea then that this grim little block was about to become ours or see that journeys are made in steps and this property would be one magical stepping stone along our way.

That night we received some totally unexpected financial help and for the first time EVER we were in a position to buy a home. We went and looked at every property with acreage within our price range and none of them appealed. Each day we would drive back down our road and sit at the gate of that forlorn looking house and imagine. *If we planted trees it could look better, if we painted it another colour and got rid of that awful beige it could look OK, but it's so exposed the neighbours will see everything we do and trees take so long to grow!*

But there is nowhere else!

One sunset we climbed the locked gate and crept down the treeless drive to the house. We sat on the verandah for hours, listening to the tiny titters of the finches nesting in the eves, watching the McDonnell ranges pulse red with the setting sun as a flock of black cockatoos screeched past and landed in the big silvery gum tree that grew at the gate of the house of our dreams across the road. Oh, the irony was not lost! Even so, we both began to feel we could transform this sad little block and the prospect was unexpectedly beginning to feel quite exciting. The following day we gave the owners an offer $25,000 below the asking price. They leapt upon it and we got ourselves a home.

I should have had an inkling of what was to come when the day we got the keys to move in. I was sewing, desperate to make headway on an order that I knew would have me sewing late into the night for many days to come. We unplugged my industrial overlocker from its place in the shed, loaded it up onto our truck and drove down the road to our new home. We struggled up the steps with this heavy machine, plugged it in and off I went again, sewing late into the night without even a moment to dance through the rooms of our empty home.

What neither of us had realised then was that we had a stowaway. Inside one of the boxes of fabric we had moved from the shed was a potent symbol of initiation and rebirth. Our old mate the giant brown snake that had breakfasted on mice by our bed, slept coiled up under our pot belly when it was cold and been a regular if rather unwelcome house mate, had moved with us.

Even though I began life in my new home working, I felt so happy to finally have a home. I yearned to put down roots, to plant gardens and be there to watch them grow. And how symbolic that my new home had come from a conversation on the banks of the Todd as we'd watched it flow for the third time. It didn't occur to me that the mighty swirling and churning body of water that spewed past was clearing out all the old rubbish left in its bed.

As I perused colour schemes for the bedrooms and enquired about the prices of new stoves, I was oblivious that a similar force had entered my life. Just like those empty old wine casks, everything that had little meaning would be washed away and all that would be left would be the love.

This force had nothing to do with a little life living happily ever after on a five acre plot. No, it was so much bigger than that. It was a life lived without limits, as big as the beautiful blue sky. It was the deep connection I felt with our earth as I ambled along tracks that wove like red ribbons through the bush. It was in the cries of the pale pink Major Mitchell parrots with their cocky bright orange plumes as they landed in amongst the paddy melons for a right old feast. It was in the lone camel tracks, like big hearts that crossed our paths when we walked our dogs and told us a wild camel had also passed this way. It was in torrential rain after a long dry season and dark skies full of dust. It was in campfires and billies boiling and diamond nights glittered with stars. It was in waking sleepily in a swag with the fire burnt to embers and the grass all laced with dew while the bright red sun birthed a new day as it bulged over the horizon, and it was in the flocks of emerald budgerigars that swooped and chattered and flew through the sky, as one.

It was the chant and the soft hum of the desert and she was creeping into my bones.

Three

Pure Happy Heaven

After my initial meeting with Abdul and my abhorrence of his species I was astounded at how quickly our lives became interwoven with our little Kunkaa and Jianti's. We loved our camels with a passion, but even love doesn't come close to what we felt. We were besotted, addicted even. The moments we spent with them were pure happy heaven. Nothing else mattered and when we were not with them, they were more or less all we talked about.

Even so I was not ready to let go of everything and head off into the desert on a camel adventure, which was what Gill kept urging me to do. The more time we spent with our camels the more dissatisfied with the rest of our life Gill became and there were times I felt really uneasy. It hadn't taken him long to feel restless with our life in the five acre burbs.

My gentle bushman resented the endless slog our days had become just to pay the bills and he wanted to sell the house and head off with some camels. I was adamant I wouldn't sell the house. It was the first home I'd had for ages and I was not prepared to let it go. I wasn't even prepared to negotiate.

Of course, I'd had an inkling that the camels would guide our lives in a totally new direction and even though my belly did flips of excitement and I could already feel the wind blowing freely through my hair at the prospect of desert adventures - I wanted both. Camels and a home. Gill however was already rolling up his swag, excited and ready to follow the camels wherever they led.

When he suggested we buy some mature and trained camels so we could go away with them at weekends and maybe take a week out now and again, I was hopeful that this could be a happy compromise. I felt desperate to find a solution that would make us BOTH happy but I had no idea that the deeper we went into the camel world, the harder it would become for me to continue to resist the flow.

Within days of our decision to expand our camel family, we found ourselves bumping down another corrugated red dirt road, this time to meet an experienced cameleer called Lee, who lived on an aboriginal community several hours away by car or three days walking with camels, who had camels for sale.

I don't know why but I'd imagined the camels Lee had for sale would be in a yard, and I was surprised when Lee jumped into our car with us and began giving us directions to his herd. He told us that the recent rains had been so heavy, the camels had gone to higher ground so it may take a little time to find them.

We drove along a really rough and seldom used dirt track, splattering the sides of our small 4WD with mud as we veered around giant puddles that blocked our way. Progress was so slow on the rough road and I had begun to wonder if we would ever get there when Lee told us to pull over and park. He then explained we were at the foothills of men's sacred country. Women were not allowed. I would have to sit and wait while the men went on an adventure to climb the hills and find the camels.

I watched them walk off into the heat haze and the salt bush, getting further and further away until they finally disappeared. It was steamy after the recent downpours and very humid. I sat sweating in a cloud of mosquitoes under the scant shade of a young mulga tree and I waited and waited. They seemed to take forever and I became more and more impatient and irritable as time crawled by. Even our car didn't offer a safe haven. It was an old soft top Suzuki and the only place to park it was in the full sun. At least the young mulga gave me some shade but if I wasn't being bitten by mosquitos, I was swatting flies that thirstily clustered in the corners of my eyes.

The hours passed mournfully slow until finally, far off in the distance I heard the faint but unmistakeable soft peels of the camels bells. I was so relieved, but it wasn't until I saw that magnificent herd of camels weaving their way through the bush that I knew every hour of sun-baked, insect infested, sweat dripping hardship had been worth it.

Most people only ever experience domesticated camels, kept in small yards and living their lives without ever rolling in a dust hole or eating bush tucker from the land they roam and it can be hard to get a sense of their majesty.

Standing out in that wild and ancient land, in that red and rusty desert where the salt bush and young ruby docks grew plump from the rain and every puddle crinkled and sparkled with light, watching those camels come in was an experience so holy, I fell to my knees in awe.

They wove their way towards me, looking like some long lost ancient tribe. They wore the landscape in which they lived and many were caked in mud that had dried hard, giving them an armadillo appearance. Stuck into the mud and hanging from their tatty and moulting winter coats were seeds and feathers, bark and twigs. They could have been gathering for ceremony, coming down from their retreat in the hills, adorned in their tribal paint, the melody of their bells clanking and chiming like some soft and ancient sacred chant.

There must have been about thirty of them and the whole hierarchy of the herd was present. There were mothers with their udders full, their young calves romping playfully beside them. Others were sleek and muscled and fit, but there were also those that looked worn thin from too many hard years in the desert and even with all the fresh green shoots it would take time to plump these camels up. In front of the herd, leading the way were a group of elders, the wise matriarchs, heads high in the air, regal and proud.

And keeping an ever-watchful eye on his herd was their protector. A giant bull, the pungent and muscled king.

It was a sight I will never forget.

A few weeks later we got a lift back to pick up the camels we had chosen. We planned to spend three days walking them the hundred kilometres home.

Lee's camels had all been named after the aboriginal children who had been the first to spot them when they were born. I knew that if Lee hadn't had a bad back he would never have sold Neville, one of his favourites, with his beautiful long slender face and shaggy deep red coat.

"You can fire a gun off him, he's that quiet," he'd told us and whilst I could never imagine us doing that, with little experience I was grateful to be buying a camel that was so quiet. Even though our young camels Kunkaa and Jianti were still very small compared to Lee's full-grown camels, they could be boisterous and unruly if they didn't get a firm hand and I had a lot to learn about setting boundaries. They respected Gill much more than me. With him they were well behaved little bubs, while with me they were hooligans. I knew I had a lot to learn.

There are traditional camel procedures that would have made handling our two so much easier for me, and Gill and I tossed and turned over whether to put pegs in their noses. When a camel has a peg in its nose, you can attach a line that goes from the peg to you and that's how many cameleers control their camels. If the camel plays up, you pull on the line and they have to behave. Their noses are very sensitive and pulling on them hurts.

In our quest to do the right thing by our cossetted and much-loved babes we even visited camels that were already pegged, but even getting close to their faces to have a look provoked a lot of groaning and shying away. In some cases they were actually bringing up their cud, ready to spit at us.

You didn't need to be Dr Doolittle to see that these camels were very head shy and very distressed. There had to be a better way, there just had to be - but wherever we turned, our doubts about *not* performing this normal procedure were met with fear. We were warned that camels were so strong we would be little match for them if they wanted to run away and many said we would have difficulty handling them.

Whenever I heard this well-meant advice I would always recall my childhood. I had been bought up with ponies and horses and ridden since I was a kid and always bareback with only a halter. I would ride for miles with my friends across the local common in the town I grew up in England. Our ponies responded to our calls and our gently pulling on the halter to get them to stop. They didn't need bridals or bits in their mouths.

Maybe camels were different and maybe we wouldn't be able to control them the same way. I didn't know and for a while we went around in circles, unsure what to do and we always came back to the glaring truth for us - we would never peg the nose of a friend.

Perhaps we were being idealistic but we wanted to work with camels in a more conscious way. The thought of any animal only responding because I was tugging on the most sensitive part of their body quite frankly appalled me and I felt so liberated the day we finally aligned with our truth. We couldn't do it, we wouldn't do it and we were united and determined to find a harmonious way of working with these animals, whatever it took!

It was encouraging to see that Lees camels didn't have nose pegs. While he'd trained them all with pegs in, he'd taken them out years ago when he realised he no longer needed them. But had that been too late to undo the damage done? We certainly noticed his camels had issues of sensitivity when we came close to handling their heads, which only affirmed our choice *not* to use them.

"You've got yourself an excellent camel there," said Lee as he headed over to Neville to hoosh him down so we could put his pack saddle on. Our peaceful and gentle camel, known to nursemaid the young and care for the old took one look at that saddle and went berserk. He kicked and bucked like a wild bronco, dragging Lee behind him who hung on tightly to his rope. Always the salesman, as Lee flew past us once again, almost airborne but still clutching onto the end of the rope, we heard him say, "He's a good camel this one, just needs a little work!" I was horrified - we had paid cash for a camel that didn't even look trained. I didn't know Lee well enough to trust that he would give us our money back. It was only when Gill jumped in to help that they managed to settle Neville down. Lee looked over at me, he must have seen the worried expression on my face. He was sweating and red and the long plait that ran down his back had come loose. "See that camel over there? That's his best friend Sally, he doesn't want to leave her," he said. I looked over to the old female camel with her white shaggy coat that hung in tatters where it had begun to moult. She stood looking at us intently. It had never occurred to me that we would be separating our camel from family and friends. I felt appalled. We didn't have much cash but Lee had let us owe him for some saddles and water containers he'd had for sale. Maybe he would let us add Sally onto that debt.

"Can we buy her too?" I asked. It seemed such a shallow thing to ask when I was talking about a life.

"I can't sell Sal," he replied shaking his head. "She's getting old herself and she don't want to be moving now." I could see he was right but I felt uneasy. I had come so frivolously and I felt utterly ashamed. I had always had such a strong connection with animals and yet I had been so insensitive. However I looked at the situation I could not find any peace. *These camels are for sale. If it's not me separating them, it will be someone else!* It didn't matter how I tried to console myself for what I was about to do, I felt sick.

I walked over to Nev and hesitantly held out my hand for him to smell. He turned his head towards me. There was such intelligence in his eyes, the trite words of comfort I'd thought to say stuck in my throat. I stroked his head. I knew we were going to take him home with us and there was nothing I could do to ease the separation between Nev and his best friend Sally. All I could do was make sure that Nev never had to go through this again and I made him a vow. I told him that while I didn't have the power to change his circumstances now and I couldn't make his owner keep him, I promised that we would never ever separate him from his tribe again. At least I had that power!

By the time we were all loaded up and ready to leave, it was close to sunset. We set off leading our new camels Neville and Caroline, an older and wise cow. We had been about to take a much younger female camel when Caroline had come up to me, snuggling into my side and being so smoochy that I had found her impossible to refuse, so we took her instead. Lee waved us off. There was something wistful and lonely seeing him standing there alone, watching us as we followed bush tracks into the desert, pink with the setting sun. We were doing what he ached to do but couldn't because of his bad back. I watched him for a while, feeling scared of what lay ahead without him. Would we cope with our new camels? Did we have enough water? The weather had been so hot that the fresh shoots bought up by the rain on our visit a few weeks previously hadn't stood a chance. All but the salt bush had shrivelled and died.

Neville showed no sign then or ever again of the wild beast we had left behind and the four of us ambled through the bush in the soft sand, barely making a sound. We had only travelled a few kilometres when Neville collapsed into the sand, unfit and overweight. We were all feeling pretty stuffed, so we decided to make camp. It had been a big day for us all. As we sat around our campfire, with the camels tethered nearby, I felt anxious about Caroline. She had tears rolling down her face and her sorrow was palpable.

"I don't know what to do to help her," I said to Gill. I had already climbed a tree to get some mistletoe but it wasn't food she wanted.

"There's nothing you can do, just let her go through it. You know she's left her calf behind," Gill said gently. She wasn't a young calf- she was eighteen months old and very wild. I'd asked Lee if we could take her with us, but he'd said we'd never catch her.

"I was certain she wanted to come with us, she was all over me," I said. "I was sure it was what she'd wanted." I couldn't feel happy that we'd finally got our camels when they were both grieving over what they'd left behind.

"She wanted to come alright. Just you wait and see, I bet you anything she is pregnant," Gill replied.

"What's that got to do with it?" I asked. I hadn't the faintest idea where Gill was heading.

"Lee told me he stops interbreeding in the herd by butchering the female calves. Bet you anything she's carrying a female calf. She knows this is the only way she can keep it safe," said Gill.

I was shaking my head in astonishment. "What makes you say this?"

"It's hard to explain, but it's like I hear the camels speaking inside my head" he replied. "Only time will tell but I bet you I'm right." I wriggled into my swag and lay for a while gazing into the fire. It took me a long time to fall asleep. I prayed Gill was right, but all I could feel was the weight of Caroline's sorrow and I watched her for a long time standing there, silhouetted by the moon, looking back from where she'd come. We all slept in a veil of sorrow that night.

We got up as the sun rose. I still felt heavy, anxious and knotted up and only began to feel better after I'd been to check on the camels. Something had definitely shifted overnight - they both seemed more resolute and almost keen to be on their way. We had many miles to travel and planned to be resting up under a shady tree during the heat of the midday sun. It was imperative we rose early each day. We set off following the tree line that ran alongside the ridge. Lee had told us there were dams all along our route home so I hadn't been unduly concerned about our dwindling water supply, but each dam we passed was a muddy puddle and had cattle standing knee deep around its edge. We pushed on, ever optimistic that the next dam would be better. I wasn't convinced when Gill reassured me that I wouldn't be able to tell the difference in a cuppa when we filled our empty water containers with what looked like liquid cow poo. And he was so wrong, even strong coffee didn't hide its vile taste. But I didn't care, I was in love with the adventure we were on.

At night we slept in our swags around the campfire, the huge vast desert sky tinselled with stars. We woke early with the flocks of budgerigars, flashes of emerald chatter sweeping across the sky and the raucous screech of the black cockatoos as they settled, flashing their orange tails feathers in the gum trees we were camped by whilst our precious camels, sat in the glow of the early morning sun, peacefully chewed their cud. I could have travelled for ever, but as the MacDonnell Ranges got closer and the dirt track we followed turned to tar, our journey came to an end.

Arriving back into the world of suburban acreage with neighbours all around, back to the grind of paying off a mortgage and all that went with that made us both walk a little heavier. I could feel Gill settling back into a discontent the moment we went through our gate. My world had suddenly shrunk too, now time with the camels would be something we would have to strive to fit in and not part of each rapturous moment of life. Every step of our long walk home had been pure and utter joy. To let go of what we had just experienced, to return to the drudge, even to me in that moment appeared insane but I *still* wasn't ready to let go.

Even though I felt the cage doors close behind me the minute I got back, I was a willing prisoner silencing my need for a fuller life with tubs of ice-cream and too much wine which only made me feel worse.

I had never walked a path that had blended into mainstream before and I'd only done it now because I wanted something that everyone else seemed to have - a home! A place I wouldn't have to move from when the lease was up, where I could plant trees and watch them grow, where I didn't need to ask permission if I wanted to have another dog.

I had wanted my own home for so long and way before we bought our home I'd sat out under the moon one night and had a long phone chat with my father in the UK, Philip. We were laughing together as I humorously described the challenges of living in our old tin shed. Who else has to deal with snakes as they wake up, or being baked by the heat or frozen alive, not to mention wading through flood water to go to bed! And then in a more wistful tone I had told him that wherever I went I always felt as if I was on the outside and all I wanted was to fit in.

"I just want to be normal," I'd sighed.

"Do you know what that would make you my dear?" he'd replied and I had held my breath, uncertain what he was about to say. I hadn't grown up with my father and we had only recently met for the first time, yet we shared a deep and wonderful connection and I always found him really wise.

"Ordinary, my love, that's what it would make you."

Well here I am Papa, I've gone and done it. Whittled my life down to the bones just so I could fit in and be like everyone else, except our front yard isn't like the rest of the yards in the street. In ours we have these strange beasts with humps that get into my dreams and my every thought, calling me in gentle whispers night and day. I know Gill hears them too, he speaks with the same soft voice that entices with its promise of freedom and I don't understand why I hang on. Why I let the lines of worry etch deeper into the man I loves face, why I blanket my life in obligations so as soon as I open my eyes each day, I have to start at a run just so I don't get left behind.

Our camels want me to let go and come with them and I feel so light and joyful when I imagine walking away with my camel friends and leaving all the crap behind. I ache to feel free but I am not ready to go yet. I've only just got this home and I am fearful at the thought of letting go and having nowhere to live that's mine again. I am clinging on for dear life but the force that's pushing me to let go is so strong,

I don't know how long I can resist.

Four
Prayers Answered

I always laugh when people ask me how I got camels. While there may have been a time in the very beginning as I led my little chocolate brown Kunkaa into her yard that I may have thought I'd had some conscious choice, even that appears now as an illusion. Our two little babes were the forerunners, weaving their spell in our lives, enticing us with their charm, getting into our thoughts and whispering to us in our dreams and every dream belonged to them.

It was sweet Kunkaa and Jianti that opened the gate, but by the time Neville and Caroline arrived we were under the camels spell and they began to come from everywhere.

We had heard of one young orphan, only a couple of weeks old that was tied to a tree day and night. We knew his owner and went to see him, certain we could come to some agreement to take this little babe on. He wasn't being looked after where he was.

You know, I liked his owner. He was a tough Aussie guy with dreamy blue eyes who struggled to show his feelings, but I could always see beyond his tough veneer and so I'd imagined a different outcome from his initial response.

As polite as I was, nothing I said would persuade him to let us take this baby camel. I offered money, I even tried to tempt him with new camel blankets for his camels which I would personally make. He was adamant the baby camel was staying where it was.

I had tears streaming down my face as we got into our car. I felt so helpless. What this guy was doing was cruel, and yet he'd been so stubborn in his refusal to see it. I didn't know what to do as we drove away but I was adamant I was not giving up. An animal needed help and I would do everything I could to make sure he got that but wherever we went - to the RSPCA, even the local council - we could not rouse any support.

I'm usually a pretty gentle person unless an animal is involved and then I can be ferocious, though I always prefer to work things out amicably. That was certainly my intention when we decided to give it another go and drop in on our way home but if anything, he had only become more entrenched in his strange belief that he was teaching this baby camel to be a camel by tying it to a tree. When he began to mock my sensitivity to this camel's needs, I exploded.

"You're a fucking arsehole and you should never have an animal you can't care for!" I yelled. He went red in the face and looked a little shaken, but he didn't dare mutter a word. I was so damn mad I was spitting.

"Keeping a baby animal tied up for twenty-three hours a day is cruel!" I felt so sad that this beautiful innocent animal was in the hands of such a stubborn and insensitive brute and I was sobbing and shaking as I got back in our car, hopeless and exasperated I'd not been able to help.

By the time we arrived home twenty minutes later I was really downcast. I had to find some way to shift the way I felt. I'd not been able to help this baby camel, but holding on to my anger was not helping me.

I was on my hands and knees in the vegetable garden planting seeds when Gill yelled excitedly from the house that I had a phone call. I ran up to the house to find Gill with a huge smile on his face. I curiously took the phone from him. I was astounded to hear the voice of the guy with the little camel. I could tell he was nervous and felt unsure of himself and I did hear a slight stutter, but holy moly I couldn't believe what he had to say - it was the last thing I had expected.

"You're right Kye," he said. "I can't look after this camel properly and I want to give him to you."

I was blown away. Awed by this man. I don't give a shit that people make mistakes, we all do. We all have times we think we are right when we are not. It takes huge courage to admit being wrong and this man had my full admiration.

We jumped into our little Suzuki 4WD at the speed of light, giddy with delight, laughing at how crazy life was and drove back to his place exclaiming the entire way over the verging on miraculous turn of events.

Our new baby camel was the sweetest camel you ever did see. He was almost pure white, with huge black eyes and long dark lashes. We tucked his long lanky legs underneath him so he folded up neatly enough to fit him in the back of our tiny 4WD. I sat in the back with him, my arms wrapped around him and all the way home he spoke to me in these soft deep little grunts as he looked at me with his beautiful big dark eyes.

We were completely unprepared for such a tiny camel and failing to notice how camels were completely invading our lives and anything 'not camel' was being turfed out. We transformed our big car port into a comfy home for this calf, who we named Kushy. The car would be fine outside but our little love would not.

It soon became clear that Kushy was afraid of other camels. He would hide behind our backs, trembling with fear if our other camels came anywhere close. It wasn't surprising. Being so young, people had well and truly imprinted on him. He'd forgotten his wild roots and that he'd once had a camel mum.

Kushy had been found on an aboriginal community and in his few weeks of life, had already spent more time with people than camels. I was told he could drink a can of coke but we had no inkling to test that, and it became apparent when we had visitors who were smokers that he loved the smell of tobacco on people's breath. He would push his little face up against theirs, inhale their breath and then do a huge yawn before coming back for another sniff. He only ever did this with smokers. Whoever had cared for him when he was a newborn must have been a smoker and from the scant information I had gleaned from his previous owner, he hadn't just had one. Kushi had been swapped and bartered and passed from one person to another until he'd reached us. I didn't want him doing any silly tricks, all I wanted was for him to grow up healthy and happy. He looked like a little waif that needed his mum and he had all my mothering instincts running on overdrive.

One of the first things we did was make him up a bottle of milk and it was such a joy to hear his happy little grunts as he drank it. Miraculously, he'd survived without drinking milk but that was all changing now and somehow, in our busy lives we would fit in caring for this little orphans needs.

At this time, most of the caring of the camels went to Gill. The biggest work load in our business was the sewing and I was working so hard that it was impossible to work harder. Despite offering great pay, we could never find consistently reliable sewers to help us and many times the finished garment was returned with such glaring faults that I would be up most of the night trying to fix them.

The only aspect of our lives that felt good and put a smile on our faces was the camels, and needy camels were coming from everywhere and neither of us had the heart or the inclination to say no. I absolutely adored them and the moments I stole away from work to be with them were never enough.

Gill's work with the clothes began in earnest when they were sewn because he was the one that dyed them so until they were ready, he had more time to be with the camels. He was the one that collected fresh feed for them, spent the time quietening the wilder ones and was mother to the orphans, but he also had another project he was working on in the far corner of our block.

Despite my lack of enthusiasm, Gill had begun disappearing in our 4WD for hours at a time, always returning with the car full of what looked to me like rusted junk. Then every stolen moment he could find he'd be down the back of our property, clanking and hammering away. He told me he had found an old axle in the bush and he was building us a little wagon so we could go on adventures with the camels.

The camels continued to come. Neither of us had realised there were so many around Alice that needed help. While we lived there up until 2003, it was a central depot for camels that were caught from the wild for the meat industry, live export, or to camel farms. They were even sold to farmers who, by overstocking their land with camels, could legally clear trees they were not allowed to fell because when camels don't have enough to eat they ringbark the trees.

These noble animals were classified as vermin and got no consideration when it came to animal welfare. You could work them every day of their lives carrying tourists until they were so arthritic from getting up and down with huge weights on their backs and no one would say a thing. You could keep them packed in yards in the full sun as they waited for a truck that doesn't come and in the meantime, terrified mothers gave birth with no room to move and the calves lay dying in the dirt.

I was horrified when I heard that mother camels were giving birth in packed yards. We were half way through shopping. Our supermarket trolley was loaded up and we abandoned it to drive the twenty kilometres to the yards on the edge of town. Oh, I prayed it would not be true, but it was.

Only one baby camel was left alive, the bodies of the other babes that had given up the ghost lay trampled in the dirt. We carried the lone survivor to our car. I looked around for his mum. I wanted to at least tell her that we would do our best for her babe, but all the eyes that watched us had the same look of terror and despair and I couldn't make her out.

We struggled for three weeks with this lanky legged white calf we called Gobi, before he gave up and died. He was too weak even to be put in with Kushy who was bouncing with health, thriving on his bottles and his safe and loving routine. Gill had slept with Gobi, wrapping him in blankets to keep him warm and the only consolation I could muster was that he'd died being loved and not trampled like the others.

It didn't ease the pain. I was devastated. Since we'd had him, every moment of every day had revolved around this frail little orphan's well-being who cried out to us in a deep throaty voice if we disappeared from sight, who snuggled up close resting his head on our laps as he slept, so trusting and innocent as he watched us with his big black eyes.

We dug a hole in the garden and lined it with flowers before laying him in his grave and saying goodbye. I was inconsolable with grief.

"Come on Kye," Gill said gently. "Let's go out bush with the camels tonight. It will cheer us up."

Gill had just finished building his small wagon and we both yearned to try it out, but I was behind with the sewing. I'd let everything slide to look after Gobi. We had bills that desperately needed paying. I was worn out emotionally and physically and yet I didn't feel free enough to take a break.

"We're going," Gill said determinedly and he couldn't be swayed. He had made up his mind. "Go and get the camping gear together while I harness up the camels." It was a command!

I lit the fire and put the billy on to boil while Gill tethered out the camels. Kushy, still our beloved bub, settled himself down in the dirt beside us. We were only a few kilometres from home but in another world entirely. Families of zebra finches with their tiny cheeps were nesting in the acacias that grew all around us. It was a sound so resonant of the time we'd sat late afternoon on the veranda of our unbought house, listening to the finches as we wondered if it would be possible to fold back the corners of our lives and fit neatly into a five acre suburban block. If we'd had trouble fitting in without camels, we were bursting out now.

We had suddenly got much too big for the life we were in.

"I want to go Kye, I can't stop thinking about it," Gill said as he threw another log on the fire before laying down on his swag. "It's all I think about."

I gave a big sigh. I'd heard all this before and every time Gill bought it up I felt uncomfortable. I wanted him to stop, to talk about what he was going to do around the house - anything but this.

"I like having a home, what's so unreasonable about that?" I asked. It was almost becoming a whine, I felt so defensive.

"At what cost though Kye? Look what it's doing to us." I didn't have an answer for that. I knew he was right

"We both love being with the camels. Just imagine what fun we could have if I make a big wagon we can live in and we go off on an adventure." As he spoke I saw the tiredness in his face slip away and he began to look so animated. "We can go and find a home that suits us better. If we keep trying to fit into a home that's not right, it will destroy us."

"What about all the other animals, we can't leave them," I said, still clutching at the havoc of my life as it was. Our menagerie was always growing. We now had pigeons and chickens and several parrots.

"We will make the wagon big enough so they can all come. Just imagine," Gill coaxed, "It will be such an adventure. The open road, the people we could meet. Sleeping out under the stars next to the campfire and we would get to know all the animals so well. "Come on Kye, it will be such fun."

Later that night as I lay wrapped up in my swag with our dogs snoring in their dug outs around the fire, a lone dingo began to howl. A plaintive mournful wail so evocative I couldn't stop feeling sorrowful at all the dreams I'd let go of to cling to a home I didn't even love. I was judging myself so harshly for the weak and fearful trough I'd fallen into. Why couldn't I let go? I loved so many things about living in Alice, but I didn't love the summers. They were so hot that every year I swore it would be my last. I could imagine living somewhere that would suit us a lot better. *Why, why, why, Kye? Just let go for God's sake*. But I couldn't, even though it made no sense to me, I just couldn't.

As I finally drifted off to sleep the irony wasn't lost on me that it was the soft melodious tones of the camel's bells that lured me like a lullaby to sleep.

Five

Gift of Love

I felt so rested when we arrived home the following day. I was still uneasy about the conversation we'd had, but the moment we got back we were distracted by Caroline.

We'd left her home because of her huge pregnant belly. The last three weeks we'd spent every moment thinking she was about to give birth and the only day we hadn't given it a thought, she had. We had left in grief over Gobi's death and returned to a celebration of new life. There, sitting on the ground, freshly birthed into the world was a well licked female calf that already emanated the haughty arrogance of her mother. It was the week before Christmas and I could not have asked for a better gift. Caroline's new born was gorgeous.

I had long since realised that Caroline had chosen to come with us the day we set of from Lee's. After her initial gush of affection I was surprised to discover she was naturally very aloof and rather disdainful. She towered above me and had never ever since that day showed me the slightest affection. If I went to do anything with her she would look over at Gill with a look of horror on her face. Her bottom lip would even quiver. *How dare he send the hired help!* She affectionately became known as Lady Caroline and with Gill she shared a relationship of equals, but it would take me two years before she finally lowered her head and gave me an appreciative sniff and when that finally happened I felt like I had won lotto. I was over the moon.

"Lady Caroline just sniffed me!" I had brightly exclaimed with a look of sheer delight on my face.

As Gill and I stood watching her new calf struggle to get up on wobbly legs, arm in arm, proud parents clucking away, he looked at me with a smile on his face and I knew what was coming. He just couldn't resist rubbing it in. "I told you so, didn't I. When are you going to start listening to me, you know I'm right about most things" he said laughingly. It was a joke, we both knew that but it was so disarmingly true. His words resonated with a clarity that left me in no doubt of the path I *should* choose. If I let myself go I could even feel a surge of joy at the thought of giving up the madness and yet it would take one more final squeeze before I would finally fall to my knees in surrender. I could hear the voice of my mother muttering, *Oh Kye, why are you so stubborn?* Even I couldn't answer that and its only in hindsight I know that letting go is much easier than holding on.

By the time Christmas Eve came, Gill and I were so broke that nothing festive had made it into our pantry and I felt really glum. The countryside around us had experienced such a prolonged drought that the fresh bush tucker we had regularly collected each day to feed our camels, hadn't come up in the dry. We'd been forced to buy hay at massively inflated prices and our weekly hay bill was more than our mortgage. I had tears rolling down my face as Gill and I hunted through our pantry to see what we could find to eat. All we had were a few jars of beans and lentils that had sat for years at the back of the pantry shelf. We were just consoling ourselves with the fact that at least we had a good pile of hay when we heard a car horn tooting from the driveway.

It was late in the afternoon and we were not expecting anyone especially *not* the person we saw getting out of their car. One of our dearest friends Nettie, who lived fifteen kilometres away was walking towards us with a huge smile on her face. She gave us both a big kiss, squeezed my arm affectionately and led us to the boot of her car, telling us she had bought our Christmas present. I could not believe my eyes. Bags and bags of shopping! Everything from the necessities of dog food and toilet rolls to fresh fruit, yummy bread, olives and gourmet dips and there was even a couple of bottles of red wine! That whole year of struggle suddenly unravelled. I crumpled under this act of love and blubbered like a baby. I was so overwhelmed by this gift. Not only that a friend had stretched their own inadequate budget to help us, but that Nettie, who had panic attacks if she had to drive somewhere new, had also pushed past her own fears to drive out to see us - something she had never done before. We had met Nettie when she became our book keeper and from that moment on I knew she would become a treasured friend. She had spikey bleached hair and a cheeky smile and exuded such warmth. She hadn't needed me to tell her about our financial woes, she kept our books. It was there in black and white.

I hadn't realised I was so loved and suddenly that was all that was important. LOVE. What the fuck had I been doing? I was so close to losing Gill, we were in so much debt, our life had become a burden. We shared a love few others had and most desired and yet I'd been willingly watching the magic between us fade and almost die.

And as if all that wasn't enough to have me sprinting down our driveway with a huge FOR SALE sign to tack to our gate, I got the final wakeup call loud and clear a week later.

It was New Year's Eve when we saw the crow. We had just dragged a big pile of wood over to build up our camp fire. On the back of one of our chairs sat her royal highness Juji, our naughty corella parrot. She had come to us with a reputation of biting and while she did that on cheeky occasions she also kept us entertained and laughing with her antics which included singing and laughing and answering anyone's call to see if we were home with a loud 'hello'.

Juji often joined us on camel adventures and was always present at family celebrations, as were our five dogs that lay slumped sleeping in the dirt with Kushy. It was an endearing scene for anyone unfamiliar with our lives, but for us it was fast becoming just the way we lived our life. Always in the midst of a bevy of happy animals.

We had made it to New Year's Eve with the food that Nettie had bought us and all we had left was that last bottle of red wine and a few snacks. As we sat by our fire, we could hear neighbours, up and down our street, gathered to party and drunkenly cheer in the new year. Gill poured us both a glass of wine, though what we were celebrating was unclear. Another year like the last one? I just wanted to cry. We'd barely had a sip from our glasses when we noticed something dangling from a tree just within reach of the camels who were leaning over the fence, stretching as far as they could to give it a curious sniff. "What an earth is it?" I said to Gill, getting up to go and take a look.

Hanging upside down from a length of twine was a crow. I can't even imagine how this bird had got in such a tangled predicament. The twine wove round and round his legs, even between them, binding them tightly together. Gill got out his knife and cut the crow down from the tree and while I held the crow securely, he began cutting away at the twine. Crows have always been powerful messengers for me and what a slap in the face it was seeing my life mirrored in this crow's entanglement. All the trite and meaningless things I had held onto that had prevented *me* flying free. I had bound myself up well and truly!

How ironic that our beloved camels were all around us witnessing the moment I finally reclaimed my sanity. I am sure they sighed with relief as the cut strands of twine fell onto the earth, freeing up the crow and the last of my resistance, finally, slipped away. Even though I loved my camels with a passion it was the direction they were guiding our lives in that I'd resisted. I wanted them in my life, but I was scared to let them fully in. It was like wanting to swim in a crystal clear creek but only putting my big toe in the water. Now I was ready to dive in, and as we all stood together bathed in that golden glow of cusp light when everything looks like it's on fire and watched that crow fly free into the radiance of the days last breath, I knew exactly what I had to do.

I don't know how I had ever lost the truth that all that's real in life is the love and what's important can never be found in what we own.

We were selling up and leaving on a big camel adventure and I was delirious with joy. I couldn't wait. I felt so excited and when I woke early on New Year's Day I didn't have the slightest doubt I had made the right
choice. It had been a bawdy night and we'd sat by our fire dreaming up our camel trip to the background noise of drunken song and ribald laughter. It seemed like every house in our cul-de-sac was having a raunchy
party and I longed for the silence and stillness of being in the bush. So often our neighbours intruded into our lives whether it was their dogs that killed some of our chickens or their motorbikes going up and down our road making an awful din. Someone had even dobbed us into the council for having one caravan on our five-acre block. This had led to some suited men arriving unannounced taking photos of our home from a parked car across the street - followed by a mailed warning from the council to remove our one offending van as we did not have a permit for a caravan park or pay a

massive fine. To any sane person it was ridiculous and it felt so liberating to let it all go.

In that very moment of surrender as I had watched that crow fly free I felt as if I'd erupted from my five-acre block. I'd suddenly become much bigger and way more expansive than the life I was in and after so long playing small there was no going back. I felt elated as I sat in my swag, watching the sun rise on a new year, that had unexpectedly become ripe with possibilities. The sky was a wash of pink and a flock of noisy galahs chortled and chattered on the railings of our camel yard. Alongside me lay Kushy, my little white love, his lanky legs stretched out in the ancient red sand of the desert I loved, while our dogs were tussling over who got to lie on Gill's empty swag.

Gill had risen early to give the morning bottles to our orphans but he had barely been gone when I heard him calling me excitedly calling. "Kye come quickly, come and see this"

I was intrigued and jumped up and ran over to the house. Nothing could have prepared me for what I was about to see and for a moment I shook my head as if I was hallucinating. Life had not only sent me a tangled crow as a messenger, it sent a drove of nine week old piggies and they were climbing and frisking all over our orphan camel Munki as he sat contentedly chewing his cud, looking as if being covered in tiny piglets was just a normal thing. We laughed so much and after a while they all took off, one happy gang with their mission accomplished, scampering down our drive, hopefully home.

I have a big affinity with pigs and was born in the Chinese year of the pig. I knew they represented good fortune and fun so I couldn't have asked for a better message that I was on the right track. It was also significant that our piggy visitors had chosen Munki to visit because he also was on the threshold of not just a beautiful new life but one in which, just like us he could now thrive.

Munki had arrived in our life somewhere between Kushy and the departure of Gobi. We'd never publicly announced or even intentionally stepped in the direction of being the saviours of orphan camels though word soon spread that we were the folks to help an orphan in need. When we were contacted about a young camel living on an aboriginal community in danger of being attacked by dogs and needing to get out before he was harmed, we agreed to take him on. He was delivered to us by an awesome neighbour called Wayne who had been travelling around the communities replacing smashed windscreens. Even though the community was about ten hours away, Wayne was pretty adamant that it wasn't a problem picking this little camel up.

It was late in the afternoon when Wayne's van finally pulled into our driveway. I had been pacing with excitement at the prospect of meeting our new orphan and I couldn't understand why Wayne was being so apologetic. He looked wrung out and exhausted and kept saying 'I'm really sorry, I didn't know if I should bring him or not.' It wasn't until Wayne opened up the back door of his van that I understood. Munki literally erupted from the inside bawling, spitting green goo *and* with a really bad case of the shits that was going everywhere. The inside of Wayne's van was a big pooey mess!

There was no doubt Munki was deeply stressed but what was even more shocking was his condition. He was very skeletal, had barely any hair on his body and his entire skin was red and raw and covered in sores. 'I didn't know if you'd want him when I saw the state he was in" said Wayne. There was a moment when Gill and I had stood speechless, but not because we didn't want him. We were appalled at his condition but so grateful that Wayne had braved everything to get him to safety, even fighting of a pack of dogs that were trying to maul Munki as he was being loaded into Wayne's van. It was camels like Munki I wanted to help. We didn't have much time before it got dark and there was no way we could put Munki in his poor condition in with our other camels. All we could do was quickly knock up a small yard - a few star pickets and some wire on the edge of our veranda. That way we could be close to him night and day. Sensible parents that we were we even moved our bed onto the veranda so we could keep him company and give him his early morning bottle without having to get out of bed.

Munki was certainly old enough to do without a bottle and while it may have appeared as just an act of pampering, it was much more than that. Introducing a bottle to a young animal that's experienced such extreme neglect has more than a physical benefit. It lets that animal know that mum is finally here they are safe, they can let go and they are going to be looked after. Feeling safe and loved is an essential part of healing. I have heard people say that a young animal will never fully recover from such a depleted state and that's just not true. Well at least it wasn't in Munki's case. This undernourished waif eventually grew so big he became our biggest camel. There is no doubt we faced challenges with his health but I have always believed every challenge has a solution and each time we found it. He was such a stoic little camel who took everything in his stride without a grumble, including his daily run. Even feeding him little and often he tended to bloat after every meal. After trying several different remedies Gill discovered that running really helped. Munki adored Gill and followed him everywhere, so Gill would take off running around our house with Munki striding out behind him, farting all the way as they did their laps. They would run until Munki's bloated belly had gone down. The exercise did our frail little orphan so much good, he got stronger every day. We'd had to be relentless in treating his skin condition but after a few weeks it was so rewarding witnessing the first fuzz of new hair on his bare body.

Even without all the orphans to look after, I don't think either of us had really anticipated how much work we had to do to make our trip a reality. Not only were we preparing for a massive adventure, we had to continue running our business, finish renovating the house so it was ready to sell *and* care for the camels and other needy animals that kept coming. On top of all that Gill also had to build our camel wagon and every spare moment he had was spent down the back of our block working away on it. I wish I could say that this time of preparation for our trip had been exciting. In truth from New Years Day on our days were an unrelenting graft.
It would have been easier to give up, to stay in bed or even pale down our dream but the idea of a more simplistic goal felt like a huge loss. We couldn't do it and we didn't want to leave any of the animals we loved, behind.

There were times late at night when all the jobs were done, when Gill would lead me down to the bare bones of his wagon. We'd sit in its ark like hull perusing maps and possible routes. I could already hear the soft clanking of the camels bells as they led the way and our wearied faces would always brighten from the imaginary fires we'd light in all the imaginary places we would camp along the way. I always felt so rejuvenated from being immersed in our vision. We could do it, I knew we could. We just had to keep going.

Now I have to be honest. There is something I haven't explained, perhaps because I felt a little embarrassed by my failings in this realm. Even though I loved the camels, they often scared me. It could have been related to my initial experience with Abdul who'd *really* freaked me out. I'd had nightmares for weeks about him! I was fine with the orphans and the grown camels I knew were gentle, but even then I would always lead them at a slight run, looking over my shoulder, terrified I was about to be trampled. I was not a natural cameleer and I really wanted to be.

Kunkaa and Jianti had grown quite big and to them I was a play thing they didn't respect at all. Like badly behaved teenagers they would buck and kick out around me, always challenging my boundaries which didn't exist. Their behaviour did not help my frail confidence as a fledgling cameleer. Once, they had circled me, bucking and kicking out as I stood vulnerably out in the open. It was prankish behaviour but had the potential to be dangerous. They were playing while I was in fear for my life. If I wanted to form a relationship with these animals I had to let them know what they were doing was not ok - but I didn't. I didn't even try and stand my ground. I knew the wisdom in facing them, especially after dealing with the red rogue from hell, but I had felt so vulnerable with the two of them bounding up and down around me, I had run. It was game on and I sunk even lower in the camel pecking order. If that was possible. I may have been at the bottom anyway.

They never behaved like this with Gill. They were sweet and well behaved for my beloved, ambling along beside him like little lambs. They saved their hellish side for me. I was in no doubt that our choice to *not* nose peg our camels was forcing me to face all my fears and insecurities and grow. I could not be in my fear and have camels without nose pegs. My choice was get some very clear boundaries or be trampled. It was as basic and as crude as that. Of course I didn't know how I could change my mindset overnight, or at least fast enough to deal with our riotous camels safely. After all we were preparing to leave. I had to get this and *now!* I should have known that when you take on big challenges, you get everything you need to accomplish them, including big lessons.

We were so keen to leave, we began selling everything we owned in a series of garage sales and it was at one of these sales I got a huge wake up call about trusting myself.

Six

Forsaken Trust

I was happily serving customers at our garage sale when I noticed a couple that I knew had camels arrive. I loved to connect with camel folk, I always learned so much - but I'd never felt naturally drawn to this couple and I should have trusted that. They hadn't been there long when the wife began picking at me for keeping little Kushy in the car port. She told me I was spoiling him and he would grow up to be dangerous. "Put him in with the other camels and let him be a camel," she'd retorted.

Oh boy, did she activate a massive fear. I only had to remember Abdul and all the other stories I'd heard where the orphan ended up being shot because they were dangerous. It was something Gill and I often discussed and we both felt that by gently setting in place clear boundaries for the orphans when they were tiny, they *had* to grow up to be respectful. Once we'd even had to tell Kushy off for sitting down on Gill's lap. It was an adorable act and heartbreaking to reprimand him for it but if he didn't learn when he was little, he could kill us when he got big. Surely, we were doing ok? I didn't know, I'd not done it before and this woman's scorn infused me with self-doubt.

What if she was right? Were we spoiling him? What if this gorgeous little love with his huge soulful eyes *did* become dangerous?

I had felt *not* to rush him in anything. He was slowly getting used to the camels sniffing him over the fence. He didn't have a mum and he was too small to put in with fully grown camels. That's what I kept telling myself, but was I wrong? I fell into a quagmire of uncertainty that even Gill couldn't talk me out of. By the end of the day I was determined Kushy was going in with the camels. I led this little animal that had nothing but trust for me into the camels yard and when they slowly and amicably walked towards him, he freaked out. In a blind panic he ran straight over the top of a fence star picket, cutting himself all the way along his under belly, from his pedestal and narrowly missing his pizzle.

As I led him back into his safe and loving haven I was fucking devastated with myself. I'd only had a couple of conversations with this woman over the years and each time I had been struck by how mean spirited she could be. But what made it even worse was that I had seen her camels after one of her desert treks and they had been emaciated and covered in deep saddle sores. There was no way we'd put our camels through that and yet I had let Kushy be vulnerable to the same mean spirit. I had to forgive myself for that.

We got Kushy back to his safe haven and settled him down, never to be forsaken in trust again. He was happy once he was home but I clucked and fussed around him in grief over what I'd done. I gave him a soothing bottle and Gill cleaned and treated his bloody wound but it left a scar like a long zip that never went away. Kushy wore that battle scar, my constant reminder of the day I vowed to listen and always trust in my compassionate self.

How uncomfortable reflections can be. I had not been so keenly aware until that day that the way I allowed people to treat me, was mirrored by our more challenging camels. The lack of respect I showed myself mirrored the respect they showed me. It wasn't even about me showing them who was boss, that was a ridiculous notion and so outdated if I chose a more conscious communion with my animals. I had to start respecting myself and trusting in me. I thought I'd got the full lesson then from letting down Kushi, but a camel who was yet to arrive would teach me another important aspect of boundaries.

I named her Jumuna after the river that flows past the Taj Mahal in India and I wanted her to know she was so deeply loved and I would do everything I could to help her. She had come into our lives unexpectedly, distraught with grief.

A week before we knew our destinies were woven with hers I'd noticed her trapped within yards brim full of camels freshly caught from the wild and facing death at the abattoirs. We were passing these yards and hadn't been able to resist stopping to have a look at so many majestic camels in one place. It was her ears that had drawn me to her - they were shaped more like a mouse's than a camel but I hadn't lingered on her. We only stopped for five minutes. I felt grief at what these camels faced and was keen to go, but we were there long enough to notice 'mousey ears' and a huge white majestic camel that towered like a mythical beast above the rest. Then we got in our car and drove away without a backward glance.

And when I say, "camels got us," this is what I mean. Those two camels joined us in our dreams, spoke to us in enticing whispers, became our every thought. For three days we resisted their seduction. *They are wild. We don't have experience. We don't need any more work.* Yet the feeling to get them only intensified and became all consuming. On the fourth day we drove to the yards and bought the big white male who we named Zu, but mousey ears was nowhere to be seen.

It had taken Gill several days of working with our new camel Zu, to get him quiet enough to lead home tied to Neville and Caroline who he'd led up to the yards for assistance. In this time the rest of the wild camels had been loaded into a truck ready to leave. Only one remained and whatever they tried, they couldn't get her on the truck. She was terrified, and in a panic had rammed her head through a big heavy steel gate, lifting it off its hinges and was running out of control. It was such a dangerous situation, she could have easily broken her legs and Gill had been holding his breath praying she wouldn't get hurt. Thankfully she didn't. When she'd been freed from the gate she was herded into a small yard and Gill was told he could have her or they would shoot her, *but* he only had two days to remove her.

For two days he worked with her, trying to get her used to ropes. He had to be able to tie a rope around her neck so we could lead her out. Slowly, slowly with so much patience and gentle soothing he tried but nothing he did worked. She'd charge at Gill, kicking out violently and in the twenty-third-hour Gill told me she was not responding and he thought it best we leave her behind. Of course, I didn't want Gill or anyone to get hurt, but I felt sick at the thought of leaving her. We had an hour left and I asked Gill to give me half an hour.

I sat on those railings and I spoke to her in gentle whispers. Her eyes were darting all over the place - she was utterly traumatised, but I could see her ears prick up when I spoke. I told her how sorry I was that she'd been treated like this, I didn't know how people could be so cruel. I had tears rolling down my face as I spoke. She had teats that looked well suckled and she must have been parted from an older baby. I didn't see a wild camel, I saw a grieving mother - one that had lost her home and her herd and shook with fear because she didn't know what hell was going to be unleashed on her next. I soothed her every way I could, I told her that she would be safe with us. I even sung to her and I could see her body begin to relax. I then explained that we needed to get a rope on her and get her out. We only had a tiny bit of time left and we wanted her to be safe. She took a big breath and I felt her let go. "Gill," I called, "come in so gently now, she is ready." Gill walked softly up to her, slipped a rope around her neck and then tied the end around one of our camels. She quietly walked the four kilometres home.

I have heard some cameleers say to never waste time with a difficult camel. I even heard them describe camels like Jumuna as 'head cases' but it shows such a lack of sensitivity to even describe an animal like that. This was a camel on the edge of a nervous breakdown and we only have to imagine how we'd feel in her place to glean an inkling of the suffering she was going through. My heart broke for this love.

When we finally got Jumuna home, she collapsed. She buckled at the knees and fell to the ground and was totally unresponsive to us. Her eyes had rolled back into her head and I felt an urgency to wake her up before all her life force drained away. I didn't want her to die, not in such trauma. She had to know love, she just had to. We clapped and jostled her body to get her back into it and slowly we saw Jumuna return. It was only then that I noticed her mousey ears! This was the camel that had been calling us for days!

She was an older girl, unprepared for change and we took everything really slowly with her, or so we had thought. Six weeks later she was comfortably feeding from our hand and I'd felt she was relaxed and ready for a new step. As she put her head down to feed from a bucket I was holding, Gill slipped a halter over her head. I don't think anyone could have been prepared for her response. She became hysterical. She jumped in the air over and over again and each time she came down she thrashed her head on the ground. It was the most sickening thing

I had ever seen. She had blood dripping from her face and nothing we did in our desperation to get her to stop got through to her. She was intent on self-destruction. Finally exhausted she stopped. I was so afraid I couldn't look. I didn't want to see her jaw hanging broken and I was on my knees, shaking all over and trying not to spew.

It was Gill that crept up so quietly, slipping the halter from around her head as he assessed the damage.

"You know, I think she is ok," he said. "She is definitely swollen but I can't see anything broken."

Gill and I sat up talking for hours that night. We were so worried and didn't know what to do with Jumuna. *Do we take her back out bush and let her go? She could be caught again, we can't leave her open to that. And she wouldn't stay, she would follow our camels back home again. But if she stays, how will she cope with travelling with us?*

I should have known then to trust in the energy that had brought her to us. Like all the animals in our lives, she had come for a reason and she had something to share.

Just before I went to bed I went out to the yards to see Jumuna. There was a silver wisp of new moon in the sky and she stood looking at me from a distance.

She did look sore, her mouth was all puffy and I was about to soothe her when I found myself feeling unexpectedly angry and when my words came, they were cross.

"I've fucking given everything to you girl, I'm doing everything I can to make your life better and I'm tired. I don't know how to help you anymore. But I do know I can't keep this up on my own. You gotta meet me half way and you need to acknowledge that. I'm not doing this on my own any more." I reached my hand out towards her across the fence and held it there for her. For a moment she gazed at me uncertainly.

"Come on girl," I said, "you can do this, we can work together." I held my breath as I watched dear mousey ears with her hugely puffy nose, take tentative steps towards me to reach out and sniff my outstretched hand. I hadn't wanted anything to upset this fragile moment, not even a breath. I'd turned myself inside out to help this girl, to make life easier and happier but it was only in that moment of clarity when I stopped struggling with a burden that should have been shared, Jumuna rose to meet me. From that day on our relationship became more balanced and a subtle shift occurred in my relationship with our other camels too. Because my boundaries were clearer, they respected me more.

I still had a conveyor belt of relentless lessons heading my way from my camel friends but it was after that moment with Jumuna that Lady Caroline came down from her lofty heights and gave me an appreciative sniff. That made everything worthwhile.

I'd been anointed!

Seven

Our Love Juji

It was rather odd that the moment we committed to our trip the animals began arriving with such serendipity we would have had to wade against the flow to refuse them. We joked that word had got out in the animal realms that we were leaving on a big adventure with a load of rescued animals and so all the down trodden, foot weary, abandoned and abused beasties hobbled in from everywhere. Some even flew and it was Juji who opened the door for them.

Juji was our little rotter of a corella parrot who filled our lives with many moments in time that were so memorable you'd smile forever just thinking about them - like the time he landed in a tree at the far end of our block just as the sun was going down. He was a hilarious comedian, but a terrible flight navigator. We knew if we didn't get him home by nightfall we could lose him and we were unwilling to risk that. So up the tree we went, pulling ourselves up into its branches like a couple of kids, climbing higher into the purple hues of the enveloping night while Juji cackled like a maniac from above. We had no plan and our rescue mission turned into a game of chasey in a high tree.

I wonder if the neighbours saw us that delightful dusk. Gill and I twenty feet up in the branches of a tree, giggling hysterically, swinging around like monkeys as we tried to get our hand out of reach of Juji's sharp beak, or move a leg to safety, or scrambling to protect our fingers as he frog marched along the branch we clung to, intent on a munch. He did it all with the assured confidence of a dictator, slow and menacing except with Juji it was hilariously funny.

We hung from the branches, clinging for dear life with only one arm. Praying we wouldn't fall, unable to stop our hysterical laughter that was sweaty with fear. Only Juji could have led us into this situation that dabbled on the edge of inherent danger and broken bones and yet was one of the funniest experiences of our lives.

Of course we hadn't caught Juji in the tree. He'd flown home rather badly and by the time we'd reached the house we found him on the ground giggling away, swaying as he walked. He looked drunk but I think he'd collided with the balcony and knocked himself out. He was fine and the following day was up to his usual antics.

He had a particular penchant for biting Gill, but he always cloaked his intent in charm. He was such a manipulative little bugger. His abode was a rather rusty early settlers washing tub with a lopsided mangle on the back, which was his perch. It was from this vantage point he'd answer our door and invite everyone in, giggle, and sing. He'd rise up on his tippy toes as he performed two accompanying notes in perfect pitch, and he always joined me when I sang.

Inside the tub were all sorts of treasures. It was easy to see the cracked plastic flower pot but what else lay secreted in the murky depths, we were unsure. We'd never dare put our hand inside. Even peering in provoked Juji and the evil look he gave us was so intimidating it had the power to flatten us against the wall.

One day as he perched on his mangle, Gill offered him a cherry tomato, a feast he loved. He looked so sweetly at Gill and did a little happy dance before slowly reaching out towards Gills hand, his eyes focused on the tomato. Then just as he was about to take the tomato, the little rotter did a fast lunge and sunk his beak into Gills hand. This was the nature of their relationship. A constant jovial, hilarious power play for boss. Gill had been so shocked at being bitten he'd thrown a cup of water over Juji who'd just giggled, but his comeback revenge came later that day.

Gill had gone out onto the veranda to check what was happening with the weather. There were some big dark clouds rolling in and we were hopeful it may rain. He'd forgotten all about the tomato incident and was innocently standing looking up at the sky, a decent lunge away from Juji's perch on the mangle. I was inside the house when I heard Gill yelling and I ran out as fast as I could feeling panicked. I had no idea what was happening. Gill was yelling, "Get him off! Get him off!" Juji had leapt through the air and was hanging from Gill's backside by his beak and wouldn't let go. He was thrashing around, twisting his beak even deeper into Gill's bum. Gill was jumping up and down, flapping his hands and yelling as he tried to get Juji to let go.

It was one of the funniest things I have ever seen. I couldn't help myself. I fell to my knees laughing hysterically. Thankfully after Juji had been extracted, even Gill saw the funny side!

Juji enchanted us with his wicked and yet endearing ways. He was the first parrot we'd ever had and we fell hopelessly in love with him, bossiness, bites and all and if we hadn't we may not have been so welcoming when we heard Jo needed a new home.

We had met Jo a year before when we had connected with his owner. She was a lovely woman but if you're not soaring free yourself it's hard to empathise with the birds you have, sitting behind bars. Jo was in a small aviary but it had almost no visibility out. He had been in it for over twenty years and I felt wrung out feeling the despair that emanated from him. There was nothing I could do to help him immediately but I was always alert and hopeful a situation would arise so that I could. It took a year and the opportunity only arose because of his elderly owner's bad health. She asked us if we would take Jo and two other corellas called Beautiful and Charlie, who'd been together almost three decades and never had a chance to fly and we leapt at the chance.

We often found ourselves trying to explain why we were preparing to leave on an adventure and still taking in animals. To most people it was way beyond the realms of trust. To travel in a wagon pulled by camels with all these animals coming too. Even our dear friends would stare wide eyed, mouths open in disbelief each time they spotted a new animal. We knew they loved us dearly and were happily astounded that we could live in such a bold and daring way, but even so I often found myself justifying why I'd let an animal come. With one little doggy we'd even pretended we'd had him months and were surprised they'd never noticed him before.

I'd called into our local pound the day before to see a woman that ran it and when I arrived she was in the yard exercising one of the rescue dogs. He was a stocky little tan Staffy/Jack Russell cross and was very cute and so friendly he'd almost leapt into my arms. I'd felt an immediate affinity with him and was very tempted to offer him a home, but was I being crazy? We already had five dogs! I could hear people saying *another animal?* I could hear myself echoing the same! But why did I feel such a strong bond with him? For five minutes I had swung like a pendulum between *I'll take him, oh no I shouldn't, yes I will, it feels really good* and finally, *perhaps I'd better not*.

As I drove down the long drive to the highway, this little dog ran all the way behind my car as he tried to catch me up and I'd had to stop, turn around and take him back. I was so torn, all I'd wanted to do was scoop the little love up and take him home.

Early the next day when Gill told me he was nipping into town I told him to go to the pound enroute and pick up my little tan mate and *don't come back without him!* And that's how my little Moby arrived.

A dog who was my constant companion from the moment we met and followed me everywhere.

It had taken a lot of effort to keep our faces mute as we feigned surprise that our friends had never noticed Moby before. For a brief yet welcome moment our roles were reversed. It was us looking at them with our eyes wide and our mouths hanging open, incredulous that two people who knew us so well and regularly visited had never noticed our cute little Moby. They looked baffled, you could see them questioning their own sense of recall, all the while holding eye contact with us expectantly waiting for the first titter of a laugh, only becoming more uncertain when it didn't come. Oh, we couldn't keep up the fib for long and eventually blew our masquerade with laughter!

Of course to many, our actions made no sense. Most people wouldn't consider taking six dogs on a journey of several thousand kilometres, let alone a huge posse of rescued animals.

But this trip had an energy all of its own. Something far bigger than us was unfolding and it had such a powerful momentum. We knew that letting go allowed everything to flow, yet there were some aspects of our lives that felt like old skins we were struggling to shed and we couldn't wait to be free of them. Completing house renovations when we were so eager to be gone and continuing to run a business when we yearned to spend every single minute of every day with the camels and other animals as we all prepared to leave often felt like being stuck in glue.

We ached to be free and leave it all behind but we had to sell the house so we could finance our trip and until our house was sold we had to create an income to pay for everything. We often found it hard to trust in the unfoldment of our dream when we were making mundane decisions on what colour to paint the bathroom, or whether to go with stainless steel in the kitchen, or the latest batch of sewing - all necessary for urgent orders had all come back with major flaws.

It was exhausting. When we were tired it was easy to think we were fools with a crazy vision, but each time we welcomed an animal or Gill found some time to work on our wagon, or we sat late at night perusing maps as we contemplated possible routes, we lit up, we shone from inside. Everything felt incredibly right and we had no doubt that however big our dream got, we'd be fine.

But even we didn't have an inkling of how big our adventure would become, or that the animals already with us were only half of those that were yet to come.

There were a lot more needy critters heading our way!

Eight
We Begin to Dream

We were so hungry for the life that awaited us beyond the garden gate, but it took us nearly a year before our home was even ready for sale. By the time all the renovations were over Gill had practically finished building the wagon. The whole structure was complete but we needed to sell our house before we could afford the finishing touches.

When he had wooed me with the promise of a comfortable wagon with enough room for the animals, I had not anticipated or even imagined how extraordinary his wagon would be. Not only was it the most beautiful ark like shape, Gill had anticipated and created for all our needs as we travelled.

When we had first moved into our home we had rescued a rooster from becoming a chicken curry. A neighbour had told us if we caught the rooster before he did, we could have him. It had taken us three days of devising ingenious plots and tricks to catch this feisty and rather cunning rooster and over the years he'd become a part of our family. He was magnificent huge red rooster and had such a commanding presence we called him 'The Colonel'. During the day he roamed freely around our garden and was always the most courteous and protective gentlemen to his nine girls.

Then for three days out of the blue, he left his girls to camp out on our verandah, roosting on the back of one of our arm chairs day and night and crowing loudly every time we passed. We had never known him do anything like this before and Gill and I had puzzled over his strange behaviour. Then one morning I suddenly got it, I saw the wagon and I saw him and his girls in it and it was so clear - I had no doubt about what he was trying to say. Our dear little love was worried we'd leave him behind. "He wants to come on the trip," I told Gill, "and he wants to bring his girls." As soon as The Colonel realised I'd understood, he jumped down from his comfy armchair and returned to his girls in the garden.

While Gill had assured me that all the animals could come, I had realised the impracticality of taking our ducks. They'd all gone to a lovely new home, but I couldn't remember us having any discussion about The Colonel. I certainly would have imagined taking him impractical. How would we cope in such a small space with his early morning crowing? Well we were going to find out. After such a clear message from him, Gill and I were united - he and his girls could come. In preparation for them, Gill had created a chicken house in the wagon's belly between the two huge front wheels and he'd anticipated every single detail. Our chickens could get in and out via a gently sloping ladder down to the ground. When the wagon was in motion the ladder detached and had its own storage space. Gill had even designed and created an implement with a long handle and a metal scraper on the end so we could easily clean the chickens out. Every tool Gill made fitted neatly into its own home when it was not in use. From the back of the chickens house little doors opened up directly into their laying boxes so it was easy to collect eggs and the front of their home was all made of mesh so the chickens could look out as we travelled along. We wouldn't know how everything was going to work until we put it to the test, but everything looked perfect in its design and most of all it was a space I could imagine our chooks would be very happy in and that for us was essential.

During that last year of gruel and grind Gill often led me through his scrap heap of rusted metal to show me his wagon's most recent innovations. There were never any gentle meanders to look. As we approached Gill's creation site I faced a perilous climb over a spew of rusty metal, bits of tin, lengths of steel and old wood. All unevenly stacked, blocking the path and nothing appeared to be in any order. I had no idea how he created such beauty in the midst of such chaos and though Gill assured me he knew where everything was, I often found him searching frustratingly for tools he'd lost in the dirt. And yet there in the midst of a tidy wife's nightmare was this beautiful wagon with flows and shapes that were graceful and feminine. Gill never did sharp edges, nor did he do measurements or plans, he worked with his sight and feeling and every little detail had to agree with his eye.

Yet even though she'd been built so intuitively, she felt sturdy and dependable. A wagon so strong she wouldn't even get blown over in a hurricane and looking at her ark like shape I'm sure if we faced flooding she would float and if we wanted to leave the dirt roads and head straight through the bush, built for all terrains, we could. Her tyres were so huge she floated over corrugations and while getting in her for me would with time become an art form, in those early days there was nothing graceful about it. The aim was one hand on the railing, one leg on the tyre and then some arm muscle to hoist ourselves in, though this took much practise. In those early days, before I got fit, I often found myself hanging from the railings, lacking the arm muscle for the final heave ho in, with my beloved underneath me trying to heft me in by my bum.

Inside there was a double bed with storage underneath and a cute pot belly stove that Gill had made from a small gas bottle, complete with a large ladle like tool to clean out the ash. It was so efficient we only needed to burn some kindling and the whole wagon stayed warm. Even being highly optimistic we were in no doubt this trip would challenge us physically and we both wanted a comfortable bed and warm haven at the end of each day. The roof was insulated so on hot days it stayed cool inside and we even had a stereo with some speakers on the outside. We could listen to music as we sat under the stars around the camp fire and cooked dinner, or as we walked along beside the camels during the day. One of my favourite homes though was that of our doves. They had a cute little house on the side of the wagon under the eaves, with heart shaped windows and a little door that we could easily open when we camped so they could go out for a fly.

The times Gill and I visioned and preened over our wagon were moments of pure sanity. Planning where things would go, testing out all the old car seats Gill had found to find the most comfortable for when we'd be sitting in the front of our wagon with the reins in our hands as the camels led the way. We even sat in the front of the wagon pretending we were holding the reins and telling our camels to 'walk up.' We had studied routes a hundred times and our map was already creased and torn. Though it made little sense to keep looking at the map. We didn't know exactly where we were going, only that we were heading east, closer to family and friends and from the centre of Australia to the east coast there were only a few very long stretches of road.

Our big adventure was certainly gaining attention and we had some wonderful women visit us as a result. They'd first visited when Munki came into our lives and each time they arrived I felt as If I'd been caught in the spotlight and exposed as a mad woman. They were so deeply grounded they had the energy of ancient trees. In their presence I was always aware how scattered I'd become. I'd be organising the guy who'd come to tile the bathroom, trying to remember to order more fabric and see if Sue could work at the weekend, while remembering to pay the phone bill and draw money out for wages while trying to stay on time with making up giant bottles of milk for our orphans and tending to their needs. It was the camels that these old ladies first came to visit.

They always just appeared. I would never know when they were coming and often it would take me a while to notice they had even arrived as they never announced it. I may just glance out the window and see, almost like an apparition, a circle of old aboriginal ladies sitting in our garden on the red dirt. You couldn't miss them they were so colourful and they all wore brightly printed floral dresses with the addition in cold weather of knitted football beanies. While some were barefoot a few even had long footy socks on with trainers.

I always had a moment that felt like my face hitting the windscreen of my car. I was so wound up and busy that stopping my momentum was like doing an emergency stop at 100 kilometres an hour, but I always screeched to that halt. I loved sitting in circle with these women, soaking up their ancientness, sitting with my bum in the dirt, just like them connecting with the earth in a way I knew made sense, but didn't do because I was so crazily busy and I felt incredibly honoured that they had chosen to come and visit us.

They were all artists from the Papunya Aboriginal community and only my friend Pansy spoke English. She would try and interpret what the old ladies were saying. As we sat around a fire with the billy boiling for tea the women would tell stories and as they did they drew with a stick in the dirt. It was a circle and a sharing that always felt so deeply honouring and I loved looking at the patterns in the dirt they always left behind. I hadn't understood half of what they'd said. Pansy had struggled in her slow English to keep up, but you could feel the energy and wisdom of these old ladies words emanating from the patterns they'd made on the earth.

Like the symbols you see in crop circles, I didn't know what they meant but I felt them and on some ancient level I understood. I loved the transience of the patterns that were so fleeting, by the next breeze they would be covered by sand.

Our camel Munki had originally come from an Aboriginal community and was infamous for being the plucky little bald orphan who'd miraculously survived packs of hungry dogs and these tribe elders wanted to see him for themselves. They had all grown up with camels and it was nostalgic for them to be with them again. Pansy laughingly told us one day about an experience many years ago involving a big white bull camel. She was at a very small hole in the rocks where she knew there was water, but the opening was so tiny she couldn't put anything down to scoop up the water so she found a leafy branch. By dipping it into the hole she was able to trickle water from its wet leaves into her billycan. It was a slow process and she had only gathered a small amount of water when she heard the unmistakable bellowing of wild camels and they were heading to where Pansy had left the children playing. She ran down to them as fast as she could and gathered them all up. The only safe place she could find to put them was in the branches of a giant white gum tree. Pansy told us that the tree was so full of children, they looked like some funny looking fruit.

They had all sat safely in the tree until the huge white bull camel had herded up his girls and gone.

Pansy didn't appear to have been frightened by or put off camels and was just as enthusiastic to meet ours as the old ladies were, but Pansy had transformed many fears in her life. I remember her telling us that she saw her first white person when she was sixteen and it had terrified her. She had no idea why they were so pale and thought it could only be because they'd been drained of blood. Yet despite her initial response, years later she would find herself married to a white man and happily patting camels.

I loved these wise elders but what I cherished most of all was the respect they held mothering a baby animal in. From the day they saw me walking towards them with Munki's giant bottle of milk they called me 'Munki's Mum'. While I'd only heard them speak their native tongue they must have understood enough English to honour me with this title. If ever I was in town and they spotted me they would call out, "Eh Munki's mum, there's Munki's mum," and always with deep respect.

One day Emily, one of the old ladies, turned up by herself and she informed me by using gestures and showing me her spinning stick that she had come to teach me to spin. We had never had any discussion about this - I hadn't even expressed an interest but I felt so deeply honoured that she had chosen to spend the day with me teaching me this skill. Now I have to confess, I am NOT a spinner. I hate doing stuff like that. I don't have patience, I love creating with wool but the last thing I ever want to do is spin it. Give it to me already spun please!

I sat there for hours and could not grasp the simple technique she was using to spin some camel wool of ours. She held a spindle in one hand that she was turning to wind the wool on, while simultaneously rolling the unspun wool across her leg with her other hand. Despite me botching up every attempt, breaking the thread, getting confused as to what I had to twiddle and what I had to roll, Emily continued spinning patiently as if we had all the time in the world and there was no rush for anything.

Then Gill appeared. I was relieved to see him though I didn't realise he would show me up so badly. He literally glanced at what Emily was using to spin the wool, disappeared for five minutes and came back with a mulberry twig that he'd whittled into a spool and then he sat down with Emily and began spinning wool as if he had done it all his life! Emily's face broke into the biggest toothless smile when she saw what Gill was achieving after twenty seconds practise.

As Emily had gone to leave I had taken her into my sewing room and shown her a huge bundle of clothing that was tied up in a sheet. It was our $10 pile for the market and full of amazing bargains. A beautiful rainbow top with a tiny hole, or a fantastic gothic dress with a really small flaw in the fabric. I threw a lot of creations in that we could have sold for a lot more, but I loved having a pile of clothing that everyone could afford. I'd said to Emily, "If you would like to take anything, please help yourself," and then I'd left her to rummage through it. Five minutes later I looked out of my window and saw Emily doubled over as she carried my entire ten dollar pile away on her back. There were about forty different items in the pile.

Gill and I had stood there for a moment, wondering if we should say something or try and retrieve some of it and then decided it was a great lesson in being clear - I had after all told her to help herself and anyway, we were leaving. It was a lot less stuff to sell.

It was only a week later when we ventured into town we saw that Emily had given us the best investment of our money in smiles, laughter and joy. Aboriginal people everywhere were wearing our rainbow clothes. One little old lady was wearing a skirt as a strapless dress, there were little girls with runny noses and matted hair twirling in kiddy's rainbow fairy dresses. We even saw an old bloke wearing one of our tops with one of our rainbow headbands wrapped like a turban around his head. It was deeply rewarding to see our clothing being so enjoyed and shared so widely.

We had the biggest smiles that day.

Nine

You Will Be Guided

There were so many things I loved about Alice. I remember being a kid growing up far away from this desert town, in the county of Kent in the UK, and I had read Neville Shute's book, 'A town like Alice'. While I barely remember the book it had left me with an odd affection for this outback town and I'd had no idea that my path would eventually take me to her and I would even live there for several years, but it was always my connection to the aboriginal people and their culture that I cherished the most.

The beautiful house that we had drooled over across the road was a place where aboriginal art was created and several woman artists stayed there. It was a huge open barn like space with lots of windows and light and the women would paint these huge canvases on the floor. The entire floor would be covered with canvases in different stages of completion. These women were major artists and each canvas sold for thousands and thousands of dollars and yet they were painted on the ground in the midst of dogs, children, drinks and food with periodic dust storms that covered everything in sand.

One day I called in to see someone and was told they were out in the garden. I was guided to them straight across the most phenomenal art. It had such an intensity of power, the symbols and imagery pulsed from the paintings. The person in front of me confidently marched across multiple canvases, even leaving a trail of dusty footprints. I was astounded by his lack of reverence and politely tippy toed after him, trying with great difficulty to avoid stepping on the paintings. When I thought about it later I realised how significant this experience had been.

People come from everywhere to live in Alice - refugees, government workers, Americans (because of the Pine gap US base) and all sorts of artists set up residence, inspired by its breath taking scenery and the brilliance of its light. Wherever we blew in from, we lived every breath, every step, on the surface of an aboriginal culture that oozed from every rock, pulsed from every grain of red sand. The earth herself resonated from the tramp of all the bare feet back through time, that had pounded the dirt in dance, honouring the earth and living in a sacred way. This culture was the bedrock of everything we did and whether we liked it or not, we all walked across their canvases and we couldn't avoid it.

Oh there was definitely a dark side too. A sad and tragic side. Disempowerment, alcohol and violence and while I was always aware of that, I absolutely treasured the rich and rewarding connections I had with Aboriginal people who still lived in tribal ways.

But how could anyone *not* be inspired by living in country that held such ancient energy and such a rich culture. Alice attracted creative people. Artists, filmmakers, musicians, actors and all sorts of performers. In Summer, people went on holiday or hibernated in air conditioning from the heat but in winter, the town woke up. It was an endless feast of art and theatre and it was easy to revel in experiences that were rare and phenomenal and left us smiling for weeks on end at the brilliance of the community we lived in.

Yes, there were many reasons to mourn leaving Alice. I couldn't imagine finding a more vibrant town. We had looked to find a new home in the area, but Alice is surrounded by cattle stations and aboriginal land and it was very rare for larger parcels of land to become available. Realistically I loathed the intense heat of summer and I was ready to let that go. Change was calling and I was sure we would find somewhere else to live that we could enjoy all year round that had enough room for us and our animals. Even so letting go was not easy for me but all I could do was go with my flow and it was taking me away from this dear town in the very heart of Australia that I'd come to love.

It was with mixed emotion that we finally reached the day we hung the FOR SALE sign on our gate. A long way from leaving, it had been easy to be blithe at peoples gasps of incredulity when they heard about the magnitude of our trip, but the closer we got to departure the more fears arose for me. Gill and I were both exhausted, though Gill was always far more stoic than me and adamant we'd be fine. We simply needed a good rest and as soon as the house sold we would have some breathing space before we left. We planned to move our wagon and all the animals coming on the trip into an area already set up with water and a loo, within the huge camel paddock we leased in the airport buffer zone just up the road.

I had never worked so hard for anything in my life. Nothing had ever challenged me like this before. On New Year's Eve when I had agreed to go on the adventure I had no idea that I would need a Herculean strength over a prolonged period of time to pull it off. It laughed in the face of new age teachings that say *if it doesn't flow, it's not for you*. With that philosophy I would have stayed in bed almost every day, I would have watched TV dramas and drunk more wine as I convinced myself everything in my life was perfect.

It would have been easier if we'd put the house up for sale the day we decided to go, but it wouldn't have been wise. We needed money to go on this adventure and to sell our home in an unfinished state would have left us with very little profit. Selling our home was our way of raising funds and we were intent on getting the best profit we could. That's why we wanted our home to stand out from the crowd and by the time it was finished it did, especially with its huge copper fireplace on the verandah, its sunken spa in the garden and its rainforest bathroom.

It had been a while since Gill had built our bathtub from clay and cement and it was my favourite feature in the house. It was the closest you could get to bathing in a tropical rock pool and Gill and I could both easily fit in it up to our necks in hot water. On freezing cold days we could sit in the bath and watch videos and when we didn't have time for that, we would take our towels in and lay under the heat lamp and pretend we were on a tropical beach. Five minutes amongst the plants and the warmth and we were always invigorated.

All the renovations I'd dreamt of doing were done for someone else to enjoy. Soon, we would be completely free of any comfort zones and that was scaring the shit out of me, but there were two main issues that had me quaking with fear.

The first one was the route we would need to take out of Alice to get on the road heading east. We had driven it with a friend and it was perilous. Steep hills, sharp bends, dangerous corners and nowhere safe to pull off the road and it went for miles and miles without redemption. In some places there were sheer drops - one wrong step and we would all plummet to our deaths. We hadn't even begun to train our camels yet. How the hell would we manage this road and keep everyone safe? Every time I thought about it I felt so anxious my body would shake. Gill on the other hand was once again so nonchalant that we'd be fine and was waving aside my fears, almost as if they were completely unfounded. I could only let go. It didn't stop the fear but I took some deep breaths each time they arose and reassured myself that there was a force bigger than us guiding this trip and I had to trust in that.

My other rampaging fear was wild bull camels. We had heard countless horror stories about the mobs of wild bulls that were likely to attack our camels as we travelled through the desert. These solitary males get pushed out of their own herds by the dominant male and roam, frothy and ignited on testosterone and willing to fight you for your herd.

I'd heard of some cameleers that had trekked across Australia leaving behind them a trail of dead wild bull camels without even a backward glance, let alone shedding a tear. If a wild bull came anywhere within range of their camels they shot them dead. I knew I couldn't do that. To have to shoot camels as I travelled appalled me and yet the stories of those that had tried to avoid killing them were often horrific too. Many had spent days chasing them off only to have them return immediately every single time and after days of continued battle, totally exhausted and worn down from several sleepless nights they had finally shot these proud beasts dead. Sometimes their own camels had even been left with gaping wounds after the attentions of a frustrated and thwarted wild bull.

I had many sleepless nights over how we would cope with these bulls and while the fear did not completely abate, it lessened after some really sound advice from a cameleer I respected. He'd had years of experience travelling through the desert with camels and was one of our only supports in *not* using nose pegs.

"It's that initial moment when you first make contact with a wild bull that counts the most," he said. "You have to come at him like a wild bull yourself, none of this arseing around - you gotta charge after him with your gun, yelling and screaming as you bounce shot gun pellets of the ground. Works most times, they've just got to know whose boss, if they think they're in with a chance, they'll be back."

It made sense to me and I had often appreciated this guys no nonsense approach to cameleering and prayed it would work. We needed to get a gun anyway but even this was new for me and felt daunting. I had never even been close to a gun or even known anyone that had one. I prayed we would never have to use it to put down one of our own animals, but if we did I was relieved to know that Gill had experience with guns. We had to be prepared for every emergency and if the additional cost of a shot gun would help us avoid killing a wild bull, I was all for it.

There were some people that thought we wouldn't make it five kilometres down the road with all our animals in tow, let alone two thousand kilometres across Australia, but when you throw yourself out there in life, do something daring and bold you always get those who feel diminished by others success. Especially if you're doing it your way and breaking all the rules, pushing past the boundaries of what's considered possible. While we were aware of a few naysayers, the overwhelming response to our adventure was enthusiastic support but only a few really comprehended how hard we were working. Many only saw the romance of it all, the beautiful wagon, the Dr Doolittle scene of us all travelling through the desert in a little love fest, all talking to one another as we frolicked along - not the enduring hard labour that went into making our trip a reality.

Those that thought we wouldn't succeed hadn't seen us sitting up late at night planning, writing endless lists of what we'd need to buy and jobs that had to be done, travelling permits for some of the animals that we needed to apply for, imagining every situation we might face and what we would need. Our animals and their well-being were of the utmost importance. We would be in places we may not reach help for a couple of days. In an emergency we may not even be a days reach of doctors, let alone a vet.

And the truth was I didn't know if we would pull it off either. On days when I gave myself time to unwind, to sit in the soft morning sun and meditate, or take a relaxing bath and let go of all the stress, I felt that anything was possible and I didn't feel so bogged down with doubt. But we wouldn't know how everything would come together until we gave it ago. It was one thing to sit with a pen and paper and organise a trip from afar, but the reality of handling all these animals and trying to move together in some sort of harmonious flow was something we couldn't fathom until we were on the road and I prayed we'd get it right because our animals were depending on us.

On one of our regular market days where we sold our clothing I had even taken a break to go and get a reading with a visiting psychic. Not something I tend to do often, but something about this woman had attracted me. There was something familiar about her, or perhaps it was that she reminded me of Bella Rosa (Ghosts & Ghoumas). She felt so deeply earthed, feet firmly on the ground, a no-nonsense type of woman. I got the impression she would be blunt but her words would be true and I felt I could trust her guidance. I was aching for some clarity that everything was flowing and we'd be ok and we weren't as crazy as I felt some days. She had sat for a moment holding my hand as she tuned in energetically. I had told her we were getting ready to go on a camel wagon adventure but that was the extent of her knowledge of me. Her words when they came surprised me.

"I can see wherever you go there is light and you're lighting up the darkness. Everywhere is lighter because you've passed through. I see beautiful swirls of rainbow colours, but there's more happening than just the light - your opening up a vortex and

you have to go to certain places to do this. I don't really understand what's happening. I haven't seen anything like this before but I am being told you will be guided." That certainly added another aspect to our trip that I hadn't expected and while I had no idea what she meant I did find her message comforting.

I had these big and very valid fears about an adventure that we had pushed over the edge of sanity. Who in their right mind would travel with so many animals? When I had rung my Pa in the UK and told him of how we planned to move over 2,000 kilometres east, he had laughed and said, "Well I know my daughter wouldn't choose anything as dull as Pickfords to move," and there were days when I questioned my sanity for *not* choosing Pickfords, but what we were doing had this power behind it that we couldn't explain and without it we wouldn't have been so bold. We would have made safer plans, rehomed animals and set off with a wee team of four camels and a dog, but we were being guided. Everything lit up when we focused on the trip and when we welcomed the down trodden of the animal realms I knew in my heart I was doing exactly what I was meant to. In those moments *everything* felt aligned. It was only the grind of freeing ourselves up from the life we no longer wanted that wore us down, and it was easy to fall into doubt and fear then.

On many levels, my reading with the psychic renewed my trust in our journey. I didn't really know what she had meant but she was the only person to recognise that something very magical was happening that was bigger than the mere hopes and dreams of Kye and Gill and as someone that ached to live my life in a more purposeful way, I found that deeply validating. Oh, I wish I could say I had let go of every fear, but I hadn't. I still had heart palpitations when I thought about the road out of town, but I was more apt to rely on the knowing that as hellish as that road appeared, we would be guided.

How that would happen would come as a huge surprise, but it didn't come until we were finally out of the gate and standing fully in our freedom and from all the calls we'd received from people eager to come and view our beautiful home, that day was getting enticingly close.

Ten

Amazing Andaria

Within a day we'd received an offer on our house that we were happy to accept. We were delighted, our trip was getting closer. Freedom was just a contract away.

Now that we were completely freed up from house renovations there were new challenges to think about and one was what to do with Jo, our sulphur crested cockatoo.

In the two years he'd been with us he'd lived entirely outside of his cage. With no other parrots of his species in the area, Jo was content to fly with the galahs and we often heard him screeching from within their flock as they flew over. I always felt elated when I heard him. He'd transformed from the depressed parrot he'd been when he'd first arrived. His life was his now to do with as he pleased and most days he went on flying adventures, but he usually came home at night to sleep.

I worried about what to do with him. He was part of our family and there was no way we could leave him behind to fend for himself, but if he came with us he would have to be caged and in the two years since we'd opened up his door, he had never gone back inside. He was so timid I had never even touched him. Even when I offered him fruit I would reach my hand out so gently and place it near him. I didn't want any sudden movement to break the trust I'd worked hard to build. Each sunset when he landed back on his cage for his feed I would explain our dilemma as I filled up his bowl with seed and offered him his fruit. He would look at me so intelligently, often cocking his head from side to side as he listened intently to my words. "We love you so much Jo," I said, "and we want you to come with us on the trip but you will have to be in a cage. It won't be forever, just until we reach our new home and we will be with you all the time. I'm sure we will have lots of fun. When we reach our new home, you might even find yourself a mate. There may be other birds like you."

Gill's approach was a little different from mine. He had begun devising a series of pulleys and strings that went to the door of Jo's cage and could be operated just out of site. If we could get Jo to go inside his cage, Gill could close the door. It all seemed a little complicated to me and I was unsure how we would get Jo into the cage. That cage had been a hell for him, how could we expect him to step back into that? And Jo was much too bright to be fooled in with food. I wished there was an alternative to putting him in a cage but if he was coming on the trip, he had to be in one. He lived at his own pace, was often gone for hours and on occasions even stayed out overnight. We couldn't risk losing him on the trip.

We'd thought we were so close to leaving and were devastated when the offer on our house fell through because the buyer could not raise the funds. However, within a few days we had a second offer. We had yet to realise that people were very quick to make offers and assure us they had the cash, but the reality was that most couldn't get the finances they needed. The second offer also fell through and we were left without a buyer once again. This trend continued for the next six months. All we could do was stay focused on the animals and trust in the perfect timing of our big adventure, but it was draining. Having people traipsing through our home all the time, talking about what they'd knock out, or change or who'd sleep where. The drama of the house selling continued in the background of even more needy animals coming our way and rather unexpectantly, a donkey called Bella.

I had known of this donkey for a while and been alert for an opportunity to help her. She was on a small acreage ninety kilometres from Alice and owned by a man who was known to be very cruel to his animals. Less than a year old, Bella was already covered in harness sores. When I saw her advertised as a wagon pulling donkey Gill and I decided to step in and purchase her. It was a bit of a financial stretch at the time but it felt totally right.

As we drove into the small holding we noticed a white Saanen goat with its front leg cruelly tied to his headcollar. It had obviously been like this for so long that the poor goat had an open raw and bloody rub wound across its nose from the constant pressure of its headcollar. A barbaric act done to prevent it eating the trees. Gill and I gave each other the faintest nod, united in our intention to help this goat but we were both aware we needed to play it really cool. Not look to keen, nor spur this guy up with our judgements. When I casually asked if he would sell us the goat he began calculating his meat value and came back with the gastronomical price of $120. I had never heard of a more expensive wether.

"How about a $100?" Gill said. We'd been whispering to each other, *"Look, we can't leave the goat behind but just stay calm and don't get him angry."*

"Nup," the man replied. "I'm not bothered if I don't sell him, we'll just eat him ourselves. My wife doesn't want to, stupid woman's got attached to him."

We were standing in a yard that felt so bleak you could have sat there for years just crying and still not have released all the sorrow and suffering that permeated its rotten sheds. The day was hot and cloudless but I couldn't feel its warmth and I longed to. A dog paced frantically up and down, up and down its small prison of a yard. I was going to take this goat home whatever it cost but we wanted to at least try and get a better price. After six months of living in India (Ghosts & Ghoumas) with barely any money I knew how to barter, how to look totally disinterested, to start loading up the donkey without another glance at the goat who stood meekly on its three legs whilst its worth was haggled over. I was so tense. I could feel the frantic dog as well. I wished I could take that too and the cow. I fervently hoped he would say, "Ok, the goat's yours", but he didn't and at the last moment still trembling with rage and fighting the impulse to yell we gave in. "Ok, $120 it is," we said.

We paid the cash for the donkey and the goat who were loaded into a sitting position in the ute of out 4wd. We'd laid mattresses in the back of the ute to soften the bumpy road home for our new family members. It was such a relief when we drove out into sunshine and softness with parrots screeching joyfully in the trees. Five kilometres down the road I asked Gill to pull over. I just wanted to be still for a moment and feel the warmth of the sun on my face and I needed to have a damn good cry. My tears were streaming down my face as I told our beautiful passengers in the back they had nothing to fear, that life for them now would be kind. Odin the goat would never be tethered or bound again and Bella's life of labour was over.

For Bella it was love at first sight when she met Gill. She followed him everywhere and would have sat on his lap if she could have. When she buddied up with our dark chocolate brown orphan camel Blossom, who had tight curly black hair all over her head and the deepest husky call, they both became Gill's devotees. They obsessively adored him! I would often hear Gill out in the garden exclaiming, "Get off, leave me alone, stop it!" Gill would be trying to work and Bella would have his shirt in her mouth like some sort of kids blanky. Once I came out and saw Bella and Blossom standing one on each side of Gill and they were each trying to tug his hat off his head as he clung on to it.

Bella couldn't bear Gill even going out and every time we returned home she would not only meet us at the gate but jog along beside our car with her head inside Gill's window, braying on supersonic stereo which was deafening! Even so we couldn't stop laughing. Bella was a hilarious character and it's always amazing watching an animal whose only known hard work, break out and play and have fun, even fall in love.

Bella and Blossom also joined us on mini adventures as every opportunity we got to go bush we did. We'd load up the small wagon that Gill had originally made by transforming an old car trailer. Juji's cage would hang off the side, swinging wildly from side to side when the track got bumpy. A few young camels we were training would be tethered to the back of the wagon but Bella and Blossom, lovestruck and adoring, didn't need any ropes. They followed the wagon knowing their love was in it.

In the back, sitting atop swags and eskys were our dogs and out front we would have a couple of camels pulling. One of these was a wagon trained camel that Gill had specifically purchased because he wanted at least one really experienced camel when we eventually set off on our trip. I was hopeful of a more optimistic goal of leaving with a team of well trained and experienced camels, not just one - but if we only had one, Andaria was the best for the job. She was so bright and intelligent she made judgement calls that prevented other camels getting injured and on one occasion, possibly saving their lives.

One afternoon, we were travelling down a bush track and for no reason apparent to Gill or I, Andaria had stopped pulling the wagon and refused to budge. Nothing we did would convince her to move. We had sat there for a while clueless as to what was going on with her until Gill went around the back of the wagon and discovered the problem.

Kushy was tethered off the back of the wagon and his back leg was outstretched and badly tangled in barbed wire that appeared to be still attached to a post. The barbed wire was already cutting into his foot. If we had taken a few more steps we could have done some serious damage to his foot. He was such a nonchalant and cruisey camel, he had simply stood there with his back leg extended as far as it would go, without a moan of complaint. How Andaria had even seen this was inexplicable, we were closer to Kushy and hadn't noticed his plight.

Andaria with her extraordinary ability to see behind wagons while she was pulling them and recognise a crisis situation, while at the same time evaluating the likelihood of the humans to respond to the unfolding drama had acted without any hesitation and stopped. As soon as Kushy was freed Andaria continued down the track.

But the other incident when she responded to an emergency left me awed by the fast thinking of this camel.

Some friends were leaving on their own camel wagon trip and as the wagon crossed the road, two young camels only a few months old got separated from their mums and began to panic. Both were running down the centre of the busy airport road in peak hour. I ran so fast to try and get ahead of them but they were much faster than me. I knew I would never catch them. Suddenly I heard the pounding of galloping feet. Andaria who was on the inside of the paddock, was racing all the way along the fence line. I stood in awe watching her as she got ahead of the two terrified calves who were running blindly, panicked. When they heard Andaria calling them, they responded immediately and ran straight to her. She was then able to walk them calmly and safely back down the fence line to us so we could get them back to their mums and the departing wagon.

Without Andaria making that call to respond in such a dynamic way, those two calves could have been run over or caused an accident but what was also astounding, was Andaria was a very chubby camel and moving that fast was neither comfortable or normal yet in a split second she had assessed the entire situation and galloped past me at the speed of light. Most *people* don't even think that fast! While I do think Andaria was extraordinary I had often experienced the camels communicating with an awareness and intelligence that amazed me. Before getting to know them I, like many, had also held the misconception that camels were spitting, kicking, smelly creatures and sadly Abdul had only reinforced that perception, but the reality of these animals was far superior.

For us, getting camels was the end of life as we knew it. We had entered their world and been absorbed by them. Everything they did fascinated and amazed us, whether it was their wisdom, their humour, even their facial expressions. You didn't need to be fluent in animal communication to recognise the mortification on Lady Caroline's face if I ever went to harness her up, or take off her pack saddle instead of her equal, Gill. Her noble head would rise up into the air, so far above me and her bottom lip would quiver in horror and indignation.

But there were also times when I would notice the camels watching me and they would have this perplexed look that said *what the fuck is she doing now*!? As if they were trying to work out how I could be so dim and I often felt dim with them. As if I was only functioning on my most basic capacity. The more I got to know these extraordinary animals, the more aware i became of my own disconnection from self. I had been busy for so long, I couldn't even remember what stillness was. I felt like I was spinning out of control and all I wanted was the house to be sold so I could finally sit and be still and do only what I loved. I wanted our old life to fall away fast because apart from being with Gill, the only aspect that made any sense was being with the animals. With them I felt so happy and that had been true for me since being a kid. I'd always had animals in my life and they had given me this golden ray of sanity that had lit up every dark passage in my life since the day I'd arrived on this planet and yet I'd never really surrendered to them, until now.

Its only in retrospect I realise that surrender is a constant unfolding. Just like a rose bush whose buds unfurl and bloom before withering and dying, only to bloom again in the spring even more vivid and beautiful. Surrender is a similar act of nature. There are always more buds, always more blooms and always more deaths.

Eleven

Secret Animal Business

Lulu was one of the prettiest camels we had ever seen. Even though she was a one humped dromedary, it was easy to see her Bactrian ancestry in her squat stature and long thick shaggy coat. She would have looked just as at home grazing outside a Mongolian yurt as she did in the red desert of Australia, but this beautiful mama had lost the life she'd had roaming free. Caught from the wild, we bought her from the holding yards where she faced being sent to the abattoirs, or possibly live export.

I was certain she was pregnant, though the so called 'camel expert' who was selling her told me her full udders were due to being separated from an older calf. I wasn't convinced and my doubt was soon validated. Less than a week after her arrival she gave birth on a day when all the leaves were being blown off the trees and landing like confetti all around us. I'd watched the milk dripping from her full udders and I'd seen the anxiety in her eyes as she looked for a safe place to birth and finally, in a yard that we had secluded for her and turned into a birthing haven, little Windy was born.

We were still strangers to her and didn't want to add to her stress, but after twelve hours of surreptitious peeping, Windy still hadn't fed from his mum and had even stopped attempting to try. The last thing I wanted to do was milk this wild camel but if Windy didn't get a feed, he might not survive. I was really worried I'd get kicked but I was more concerned for this new mum. Milking her would be so intrusive and I was loathe to cause her anymore fear, but once again our camels would surprise us.

We managed to put a rope around her head which Gill was holding tight, alert for the slightest intention to kick out at me - but instead she stood perfectly still and she let me squat down by her full udders and milk them out. I spoke gently to her the entire time as I reassured her we were only helping her calf and that everything would be fine.

For three days, several times a day, we milked Lulu and not once did she show any aggression or fear towards me - but every time I milked her, tears rolled down her face. Always while being milked this mother's grief would overflow until on the fourth morning when I was just about to enter her yard, she stomped her foot and snorted, her nostrils flaring wildly. It was very clear she didn't want me coming in and when I saw Windy run over to his mum and suckle on her teat, I knew why. Wild mamma was back and just like Lady Caroline had, Lulu had done what she needed to help her calf. I hadn't even really needed to reassure her, she'd known we were helping and that's why she'd cooperated.

And it wasn't just Lulu that we'd been given some wrong advice about and from a man who was regarded as a bit of an expert. As someone that readily admitted to knowing very little about camels, I had thought what he was saying was strange but hey, he was the camel expert, not me!

When we'd purchased our magnificent white male camel Zu, we had also been assured he was a bullock and that was the key factor in whether we bought him or not. We were just getting used to camels, we didn't want to be handling a bull as well. Neither Gill or I had understood the 'experts' reasoning for why a wild bull would have been gelded. Why would you castrate an animal just so he was quiet to load onto a truck? It just didn't make sense but we lapped it up anyway. We were in love with this mythical beast who stood so tall you could easily see him in a yard full of hundreds of camels and if it meant we could get him, we were willing to believe *anything*.

Two weeks after Zu had moved in with us we were woken early in the morning by an unfamiliar sound. Our camels were humping in our front yard. We hadn't even noticed his balls drop but the following day there they were hanging, plump and proud for all to see. I am sure that Zu held those balls up while he wriggled into our hearts and then with a huge sigh of relief, plopped them down.

Since we'd sat around the fire on New Year's Eve and dreamt our vison into being, our adventure had taken off like a rocket heading to the moon and sometimes it did feel out of control. There was so much to plan and prepare for and now I didn't only have to worry about wild bull camels attacking us, we had our very own bull in our herd. How would that be? Would we be able to control him? Would he trample us if we pissed him off? How the fuck do you handle a giant bull? In every challenge and every crisis, we just kept on wheeling out that word, TRUST.

Before we'd even bought Zu, we'd dreamt about him - he'd crept into our thoughts and filled our every daydream. We had to trust in all that had conspired to bring him to us, even being told he was a bullock. While Zu was massive, he was also very gentle and sweet. We had very quickly got him used to being touched all over by tethering him between two trees so he couldn't hurt himself and gently swishing him all over with a leafy stick. He loved this and would go into a deeply blissful space. It was hard to imagine this gentle giant as a testosterone frothy bull in season. He was more like a loveable pup and Gill was sure Zu would not cause any problems on the trip.

That's if we ever made it. Selling our home was taking forever. We'd had a never-ending stream of people putting in offers and each one fell through a few weeks later. Gill and I stopped getting excited each time a new buyer appeared.

"Give it a week or two," we'd say cynically. I was so over living in a show room and having endless people traipsing through. We had barely any furniture because we'd sold everything in garage sales and while I loved living without any clutter, our hearts were no longer in our home and all we craved was to go.

One late afternoon just as the sun was setting, I was up at our camel paddock filling up their water trough when Gill arrived. He was really excited because we had just received another offer and while I wanted with all my heart to believe our house was sold, we'd been let down so many times and I wasn't willing to get my hopes up. As we filled up the water trough and watched the camels weaving their way towards us as they came in for a drink, I shared with Gill my hesitation. I didn't want to spoil his excitement but I just couldn't get enthusiastic again, not until that contract was signed.

I always found it deeply calming hanging out in the camel's paddock and we soon became absorbed by the camels and the beauty of the fading day when everything was burnished and red. Filling the water was our nightly ritual and the camels always came in to greet us. We would often grab a leafy branch and begin gently thwacking the camels around their legs, on their bums and across their sides with the whippy branch. They loved us doing this to them and if Gill and I kept up a rhythm we could dance between about five camels each, who would all stand completely relaxed, heads dropping almost to the ground, only moving if we didn't periodically get back with a timely thwack.

On this particular night though the camels were all behaving rather oddly. Gill and I had stood watching them trying to ascertain what was wrong. Physically they all looked fine but they hadn't had their usual drink and they hadn't stopped for their much loved thwacking. Instead, they were walking away from us, single file down a winding animal track, into the bush. We had no idea why they were behaving in this way. They had never done it before and there was only one way to find out. We followed them.

Billows of red dust rose from the gentle tramp of the camels soft padded feet as one by one we walked, weaving our way between low growing salt bush and clumps of ruby docks whose lantern like flowers glowed red in the last rays of the day. Already the full moon was rising above the trees, silver and bold and ethereal. I was so aware of the pace we all walked at, steady and reverent and mindful. The camels were so focused on their destination, no usual stopping for random mouth falls of irresistible tukka or to roll in a dusty hole, or even to get that pat. They were walking as if we all had an appointment, a destiny we had to meet that was so inevitable, we didn't even need to rush.

We walked for about half a mile following the camels, who stayed in single file until they came out in a circular clearing within some small scraggy trees. In the middle of the circle was a dead tree, its limbs looked white like old bones in the moonlight. Perched on the branches with the majesty of the king and the queen were two huge wedge tailed eagles. I felt as if we'd somehow slipped into the midst of some secret animal business, but I also felt we were meant to be there. When you're standing in a circle of camels in the silvery light of the full moon and you're all facing the eagles, humble yet with deep respect, knowing that something very special is unfolding but unsure what, you can only trust in what you feel.

Nothing in our lives had prepared us for this moment or given us any wisdom to make sense of it, but as I stood in this sacred circle in the wise gaze of the eagles, I was aware of all my doubts and fears slipping away. I felt like a warrior woman in a tribal initiation and I knew Gill and I had been summoned there because of our impending adventure with all the animals.

The eagles not only filled us with strength, they reconnected us with our trust in what we were about to do, our acceptance of its divine timing and the knowing that we *could* do it and we *would* be guided.

I had often felt flaky when I told people that our trip was guided. Most didn't really understand what I was talking about and I found it hard to even explain. It wasn't as if an angel had appeared in our garden and given us this vison and told us we would be guided to the promised land. No, it was much more subtle than that. In all honesty, perhaps my only reason for explaining was that without knowing that we were in sync with some holy force that was overseeing everything from above, we appeared absolutely crazy.

We often felt as if we were being swept along in a vision that was way bigger than us, but the utter hard work of manifesting it and then the frustration of waiting for the house to sell did bring up our doubts and have us questioning our sanity. No sane person dreams up a trip with so many previously abused animals coming along. Why would you make travelling in a wagon a feat of endurance when it could be a laid back and relaxed saunter with a couple of camels and a dog? We had let go and embraced this trip and its magnitude because when we spoke about it, dreamt about it, prepared for it or welcomed animals that were going to be part of it, we felt as if we were plugged in to a power socket and were lit up. We were on our path and this adventure was part of our destiny. When we felt like this it was easy to trust but when we got tired, or caught up in the emotional havoc selling our house had become, it was easier to let the fears build momentum. Many times, I swung like a pendulum between trust and fear.

As we walked away from the eagles I felt so clearly that everything was on track. For the first time in a long time I had completely let go. I knew everything was unfolding in divine timing and we would leave on this trip at the exact moment we were meant to go. I had even let go of all my stress around our house being sold. If the offer fell through, it fell through and that was fine. Our house would sell at the perfect time and for everything to unfold and for me to maintain my peace of mind, it was time for me to let go of thinking I could control everything. The truth was I had barely any control over anything.

Our latest offer did fall through, but within a couple of days we received a new one and this one was for cash. The new buyer asked if we could vacate our home in a week. After all that time yearning for our home to be sold and dreaming of the day we finally got to walk out the gate, one week felt as if it was cutting it really fine.

We asked for three and we got ourselves a deal!

Twelve

We Finally Shut the Gate

As soon as our departure from all known comfort zones became terrifyingly imminent, my anxiety about the road out of town once again began to loom. I even had heart palpitations at the prospect of travelling it as we made our way out of town.

Once again, we went on a driving foray to check on the hazards of the nightmare road and to see if at *any* point there was the faintest glimmer of hope we could safely tackle it. There were no glimmers of hope and every time we drove it, I found more reasons to quake with fear and yet Gill remained optimistic that we'd be fine! As much as I loved my man I was beginning to think that if he'd been present when the Titanic sank, bobbing around in water with his head barely above the waves, he would have still been imparting encouragement and positivity that everything would work out fine.

Yet despite Gill's infinite trust in our capabilities or even in the knowing that everything in our lives was constantly affirming we'd be looked after and guided, I'd arrived home feeling completely downcast. Some of the bends were so dangerous, one wrong step could have us and our wagon with all our camels and animals hurtling off the edge of the road into some deep gullies below. It was fucking awful and the only other option was straight through town and up a main highway busy with road trains. We had one friend who'd travelled this route in a camel wagon but he'd had far less camels than us, was much more experienced as a cameleer and all his camels were trained. I had no doubt that for the first hundred kilometres or more we'd be a walking pandemonium. We certainly didn't need potentially treacherous plunges from cliffs, road trains hurtling past, or busy concrete highways.

I felt quite desperate as we arrived home but I also felt an unease. As we opened our front door something felt wrong. A hollow silence, no 'hello' call from Juji welcoming us home - and that was unusual. We ran to his familiar abode in his washing tub to find out what was wrong. I felt sick in the stomach the whole way. Our beloved rascal of a parrot was lying peacefully on the floor, dead. Some deaths kick you in the guts and leave you gasping for air, doubled up on your knees in a dark pit of gloom. I could not even imagine a day without him, let alone a life. Gill and I sat holding our little treasure sobbing with grief, feeling so empty inside, crying so much that we were gasping for breath with tears and snot running down our blotchy faces. The agony of the pain was all too much.

We had no idea why he'd died. He'd been in fine form when we left but I've come to see over time that some animals and birds, people too, are like shooting stars. They are brilliant, so dynamic, so full of life and they often live lives that are so short but leave a blaze of light from their trail.

That was our Juji.

That night I slept holding one of his feathers, sobbing into my pillow, unable to feel any joy at what we'd worked so hard to manifest. Nothing would ever be the same again without our resident clown, our cheeky love Juji. We packed and got ready to leave feeling hollowed out, until just the week before we had to vacate the house a little and rather lovely miracle occurred with Jo.

I was in my sewing studio, packing and tidying up when I heard Gill shrieking from the verandah of our house. "What the fuck?! How the hell did *that* happen?" I ran out to see what was going on, anxious we'd had another disaster, but so relieved when I saw Gill laughing. There was Jo, sitting inside his cage with the door shut. Gill hadn't used his pulley system and had assumed I'd somehow got Jo to go into his cage. I hadn't and I was just as astounded. After two years of freedom, Jo had done the unimaginable. He had gone back inside his cage all by himself and even shut the door behind him. This dear parrot was sitting on his perch with this coy look on his face. His expression said *now surely you will know I can understand you.*

I'd spoken to him every night as if he'd understood and yet silly me, I was still surprised. While I always knew animal communication was possible, I'd never had such a clear and precise response. Jo had chosen to come with us and was even prepared to forgo his freedom to remain with us and in our lives, and that was such an honour and a privilege.

Juji had gone. Nothing would change that and while I would still cry over the loss of him and still carry his feather around wherever I went, even sleeping with it under my pillow, Jo was with us right *now*. We had to keep focused on the animals, it was the ones that were living that needed us and mattered now. I felt so much lighter seeing Jo all ready to go, sitting patiently inside his cage. It was one less worry for me. I'd been so anxious about him and what we should do and I felt such relief that this weight had finally been lifted from me.

In the last week of our home ownership it was all systems go. Gill was busy erecting a fence that would enclose an acre of land within our huge camel paddock that we could camp within. As much as we adored our camels, the orphans were like prankish kids and wanted to do *everything* with us. We needed some clear space to finish all the jobs necessary before we could leave and we still had a lot to do.

How raw and vulnerable I felt knowing that we no longer had a home. It had been so easy to dream from afar and feel confident about an adventure that up until this time had always loomed on the horizon.

We had planned to have all our camels trained by the time we left our home and beyond quietening a few down, only a couple had done any wagon work and we didn't have much time left before we absolutely had to leave. The lease on our camel paddock ran out in six weeks and trained or not, we had to be gone by then.

We were getting a lot of interest from locals - many couldn't actually believe we were about to embark on such a huge and challenging trip and I often fell in that boat myself!

One morning I was sitting in the Alice mall having a cuppa with another cameleer - not someone I hugely connected with but when you love camels and especially when you're new to them, every opportunity to share knowledge, experience, even to swap stories about our camels endlessly entertaining antics was relished.

While we were talking, a journalist I knew came up and asked when she could interview me and Gill about our trip. The cameleer I was with had scoffed, "It's not as if it's not been done before."

His sharp response had surprised me at the time. Our worlds didn't mix in many ways but we'd been having a friendly and humorous chat, so I hadn't expected his bitterness. He was about to leave on his own camel adventure walking with two camels across Australia and yes, he was right about his trip - what he was doing had been done many times before. People were always leaving on camel adventures, there was nothing novel about that, but travelling with so many rescued animals; dogs, goats, doves, a donkey, parrots, chickens, even a rooster? I didn't know anyone that had even taken a rooster let alone all the other animals.

We had one amazing and very inspirational friend who had brought her kids up travelling in a camel wagon and home schooling them on the road. At one time she'd had twenty two camels, was heavily pregnant, looking after kids, handling camels and living in her wagon and she did this by herself. She had to be one of the most extraordinary cameleers I'd met but hers had been a lifestyle, whereas we were only going on a trip.

Even so, I didn't want to detract from the magnitude of what we were doing. We had thirteen camels that had barely been handled and would kick out dangerously if we got close and while many early pioneers would have travelled through the outback in wagons, herding their animals as they went, I didn't know anyone who had travelled with such a big and varied family of animals or done so for love. We certainly wouldn't be eating our animals as we went, or making any profit from them when we reached our final destination.

There was no doubt that we had a motley crew - our latest rescue camel had arrived bald and covered in scabs that were so long they hung down underneath him like stalactites. When you looked at his face and saw his really lopsided jaw you could only assume at one stage he'd broken it and been unable to eat and that had led to his skeletal, mangy state. If he'd been in any poorer condition, he would have been dead.

In between packing, organising and everything else we did we spent hours brushing his scaly skin with a body brush to stimulate new hair. He had come from the wild and I think it was his poor condition that made him so docile. I could get right underneath him and brush the soft areas where his legs joined his body and his scabs were at their worst.

We called him Mozzee. He took everything in his stride and was always happy to trundle along with whatever we wanted to do. He loved all the attention and even had a sense of humour.

One morning when I was giving him his daily skin pampering, Gill had bent down behind him to pick something up. Gill's bum was right there in line with Mozzees foot. Honestly, this camel had a smile on his face as he gently lifted his foot and gave Gill a wincey little tap on his bum that sent him gently face first into the muck. There had been nothing aggressive about this act - it was done with humour, softness and care and had both of us laughing hysterically. Our Mozzee was such a love and he was one of the many misfits and rejects of the camel world that we were going on this big adventure with.

I felt like an emotional wreck as the last days in our home approached. For so long I'd ached to go, yet the prospect of leaving all the gardens and trees we'd planted and nourished through -10 degree celcius winters and baking hot boil-you-alive summers was heartbreaking for me. I always bond with the plants I grow. It's a relationship for me like a dear friend.

Exhaustion didn't help. I felt so vulnerable and raw as if I was being tossed out into the world naked and bare and unready, but the day approached when our very last act was to drive out our gate and shut it for the very last time, even though I was crying I was unravelling with relief.

Even Munki hadn't wanted to leave. Home was his little haven off the edge of our verandah where he lived so close to us he could even hear us snoring at night. Life was changing irrevocably for us all.

We had tied Munki's rope to the back of our 4wd with a few other camels so we could drive really slowly with them up the road to our new home in our camel paddock. The rest of the camels were already there. Despite us wooing and cajoling him, Munki pulled back against the rope the whole way. I am sure if we had undone his rope he would have run all the way back to what was once our home. We were taking him so far outside his comfort zones and there was nothing we could do but be gentle, kind and patient. We'd noticed how all our orphan camels became very fixated on routine and everything being regular and now, just like us, our Munki was feeling vulnerable.

We were almost at the camel paddock gate when Munki decided he'd had enough and laid down behind the car in the road! He didn't want to go any further. Every car that passed us slowed down to look at this unusual scene of our camel laying as if dead, completely ignoring all our attempts to get him back on his feet and moving. We were only steps away from our camels paddock gate. We talked to him, coaxed him and coerced him and it took us half an hour to get him back up. There was nothing physically wrong with him, he just didn't want our lives to change. Munki wanted everything to return to the safe familiarity of our normal life and I couldn't give him that. I knew he'd be ok. We just had to get him into the paddock and he would soon see that all our lives would be even better.

And even though I was so exhausted I could barely see and I felt like collapsing onto the road with him, I knew that if we could all just take a few more steps, we would finally be living the life we had worked so hard for.

Thirteen

Life under the Gum Tree

Our new home was beautiful, far away from any neighbours and very peaceful and serene. The wagon was parked under a giant gum tree and I could laze in bed and watch the willy wagtails dancing around the camels faces, gobbling the flies that landed near their eyes. While the wilder camels wandered away from our camp, the orphans all stayed much closer to home. Munki was slowly integrating with the other orphans but spent a lot of time hanging out with us in the inner paddock. Every night he sat with us around the camp fire and Gill often sat with his back up against Munki, using him as a back rest as he worked splicing ropes, sewing harnesses up or just eating dinner. The only other orphan who had not joined the camels was Blossom. She was Bella the donkey's best friend and the two of them, always up to mischief, were inseparable.

Even though we'd previously lived on a five acre block it had had such a suburban feel. There was a wildness about our camel paddock that was rejuvenating. I loved the silence and the way our life had suddenly simplified. Our stove was now a camp fire and our TV was the flickering of flames as we sat under skies strewn with stars and actually talked with one another instead of staring at a screen. I had spent years sitting at an industrial overlocker, or up late at night busy at a computer screen. All of a sudden I found myself tipped out in nature, unplugged - and I was so aware of the vibrations from screens and machines that were still rocking my body. I hadn't realised how disconnected I'd become from nature, stillness and my own inner peace until I found myself living in our wagon, in nature, with all our animals around us.

Often as the sun set, flocks of red-tailed black cockatoos would sweep across the sky, filling the air with their ancient squawks. It was always such a gift, when on a walk with the dogs or a trip to gather firewood I would find some of their fallen scarlet feathers, lying on the red dirt earth like precious rare flowers.

We were aiming to leave before the winter passed us by and the heat set in. Travelling in the harsh Australian climate through the summer was not an option, so it was essential we got ready to leave as soon as we could. We gave ourselves a couple of weeks to catch up on sleep and recover, but then we had to get focused and organised because we still had so much to do and if we didn't get it done in time, there would be no trip for us this coming year. We had to get busy and soon.

In the middle of our camp grew this beautiful eucalyptus tree and we set up my sewing machine and a big cutting table underneath it. It was essential we got our wagon weatherproof - the weather was already very cold and even with the fire going inside, it didn't stay warm.

We bought metres of bright blue canvas for the windows and doors of the wagon, all to be sewn into shape with clear vinyl windows sewn in, all press studded and zipped into place. It was only on our final trip back to the shop for a last few metres of canvas that we were given the good advice to remember that it shrunk quite a bit. There was nothing we could do. We'd already sewn it up and fitted it in place, making windows that could be rolled up when the weather was hot and rolled down and press studded shut when we wanted to stay dry or warm. It looked fantastic, but we didn't know then we would spend the whole trip bursting press studs as we tried to stretch shrunken canvas back into place. It sufficed, but it was disappointing to have worked so hard, done such a fantastic job, only to be given some majorly important advice in the last hour.

From the bright blue canvas leftovers we made jackets for all our dogs that were lined with fleece. They looked like they were part of a football team running out onto the pitch when we went for our daily walks, and each night with the chill of winter settling all around us, they would line up enthusiastically to have them put on.

Every headcollar we had for the camels and all their hobble straps and harnesses were lined with recycled sheepskin. It was all extra work but we were willing to do what it took to make sure everything we used was as comfortable as possible for our animals and most importantly, did not rub them.

We even had an extensive medical kit with all the basics like bandages, antiseptic powders and butterfly clips as well as our own kit for natural healing with ascorbic acid, sulphur, slippery elm powder and our herbal mange treatment. We even had enema kits. We could cope with most medical emergencies and in true Kye and Gill style we were even well prepared for motherless babes we met along the way with sacks of calf formula and joey milk.

The list of jobs to be done was so lengthy. There were rain water tanks to buy and fit under the belly of the wagon, a generator welder for any for repairs we needed to make along the way, solar panels and batteries, digital cameras and video recorders and an updated laptop computer to handle the video files.

As Gill worked on finishing the wagon's brakes, I painted the wagon with a trail of golden camels, bright flowers and twisting vines. We'd have the camp fire blazing for warmth and the music turned up loud on our new wagon stereo, lifting up the tempo of our weary tread as one of our favourite Australian bands 'The Waifs' played.

'People who think they can, I want to be just like those that think they can, I want to be not so far away from where I'd planned to be by now.'

To get through all the jobs, Gill and I often worked late into the night and there was one thing that was becoming blatantly clear. If we wanted to get away on our adventure we had to set some boundaries. People were coming from everywhere to see what we were doing and only a few came with the intention of making life easier and helping us in some way. Those rare gems would arrive with dinner all cooked for us, or came prepared to sit around the fire and glue sheepskin into the camels hobble straps, or collect a pile of firewood, or cook up a feast on the coals. We were so grateful for the givers, we welcomed them with open arms. They could turn up anytime they liked but the majority of people, as lovely as they were, didn't have a clue about giving. All they did was drain our energy when we had little to give. They would turn up at all times of day - there were occasions when I'd only just gotten out of bed and was barely dressed when a group would arrive. Some didn't even introduce themselves, they boldly walked into our camp as if we were some sort of exhibit and they had a right to be there. So many were insensitive and rude. It was driving us nuts! No sooner had we moved one lot on than another lot would arrive.

The crazy thing was that our good friends were keeping their distance because they saw we were so busy with people and they didn't want to add to that burden. We wanted *them* to come, not all the strangers.

One afternoon we sat around the camp fire with a group of close friends and hatched a plan. We painted a huge sign on the gate that was a good half a mile away. I'd let the red paint drip so it looked like a little scary like blood and it said in huge letters BEWARE BULL CAMEL IN SEASON.

Problem solved! From that day forth when we heard people coming down the track, we knew they were friends. Our harmony was restored and we could focus on our departure.

I was delighted that our scary sign had not deterred Pansy and the old ladies from Papunya who arrived one afternoon in their mini bus to catch up on our adventures. I didn't care how busy we were, we always stopped for them.

Pansy told us that the old ladies wanted to know what animals were coming with us on the trip. They were all sitting in the dirt around the camp fire with their bright floral dresses billowing around them, legs garbed in football socks with mismatched crocheted beanies pulled down around their ears keeping them warm and big gappy smiles as they laughed and nudged each other jocularly. I don't know what they'd been told about our trip because we never talked about us, and because they spoke in their own language nothing they said was understood, apart from when they called me 'Munki's mum'. So while the blackened billy bubbled to boil on the flames, we began our list of the animals that were coming with us with Pansy translating.

At first, they didn't look surprised. Nineteen camels - it was a bit excessive but they could cope with that. Six dogs - yup there were large numbers of dogs on their community but none of them wore little sporty blue coats like our pampered pooches did, that was funny. Nine goats and they began to nudge one another in merriment. I don't think any of them expected our list to continue and their mouths fell open when it did. Four parrots and they were chuckling. When we told them about our giant red rooster The Colonel and his nine girls, they were in hysterics. A rooster crowing under our bed! That image was hilarious for them. They thought the list was finished and when we continued, they were holding their sides they were laughing so much. By the time we got to the doves and Bella the donkey they'd moved into incredulity and awe, but they all left that day with the biggest smiles on their faces.

I was still freaking out about the road out of town and as we got closer to departure, the horror of it consumed me. We drove it once again with two close friends who even organised time off work so they could travel it with us and help, but that time came and went. We were still unready to leave. In our heads we'd imagined what we had to do but everything took so much longer and in truth, we couldn't maintain a pace of working all through the day and late at night.

I kept recalling those eagles and how as we had stood in that holy circle with all our camels, in that moment, I had known without doubt that we would leave at the perfect time. It was divine timing, not ours. I had also had an experience when I had sat down under a tree, released all my fears and asked to be guided. In that moment I knew that every time we needed help, someone would be there. It was so easy to embrace these truths in the moment and to know them on the deepest level, but as a 'little' human getting ready for an adventure that was taking me completely outside all comfort zones and was huger than anything I'd ever done before in my life, the fears kept creeping in for me and most of them were focused on *that* road.

Oh, it was different for Gill - perhaps he stayed more focused in each moment and didn't look too far ahead. It was me doing all the worrying. I'd let go to the flow of many huge adventures in my life but I'd never had so many innocent souls depending on me getting it right before.

I thought I would feel better if we began to work with our camels. So many were still wild and it was time to bring them all in close, get them used to being handled and at the very least, quieten them down. The sooner we began living the routine we would be in when we left the safety of our paddock, the easier it would be for us all. That date was fast looming and we had to act.

The camels had all been grazing freely for the first month or so we were camping in the paddock, growing fat on the acacia blossoms that they loved and lazing in the dust holes in the soft winter sun.

As the weather had gotten colder, Zu had come into season and he become very territorial with our herd. As we attempted to bring all the camels in closer to camp, Zu kept coming in between us, blocking our way. He wouldn't even let us get close to them to give the friendly ones a pat. He would charge towards us, cutting us off or herding them away from us before we even approached. This happened many times and we were unsure how to proceed. We had never handled a bull let alone a bull in season before and we didn't know what he would do. We even tried to herd them in the car and almost made it back to camp only to have Zu, at the last moment, chase them all back out bush again.

I had always believed that communicating with the animals in a conscious way was possible. We'd already experienced Jo going back in his cage, but had that just been a bizarre coincidence? For most people, communicating with the animals was akin to being whisked away by a knight in shining armour or coming across a house made of ginger bread and chocolates. Surely talking to the animals was as real as Father Christmas and the Tooth Fairy?

But every time I pondered on what to do about Zu, Jo flew into my thoughts.

In the dirt and the dust with the crows cackling like crazy old witches in the gum trees and a wild bull camel that was not responding in any way to our pushier attempts to gain control, it finally dawned on us to try another way. We went with our tails between our legs this time, our bullying ways all done and humbly stood in front of this king of a camel as we asked for his help. Although I had clutched my fairytale of a dream of speaking with the animals to my heart and carried it all through the years, when they finally responded to my communications, I was as gobsmacked as everyone else.

People had thought we were joking when I had told them about Jo returning to his cage and now Zu, this huge beast, all muscled and pumping testosterone was walking towards our camp, following winding tracks that led through the acacia and the blossom they loved to eat and never usually passed without reaching for mouthfuls, on past the scraggy mulgas with the rest of the camels following in single file behind as they walked the four kilometres home. When they arrived at our camp we walked up to each one, put a rope on them and tethered them to the trees.

If I had not of seen it for myself, I would not have believed it to be true. I finally had no doubt. When we chose to communicate with our animals in a more conscious way they not only listened, they responded.

Fourteen

The Unveiling

We began tethering all the camels on long ropes attached to a strap on their ankles and moving them around several times a day to fresh feed. Tethering them always mellows them out, but it takes time for them to get used to it and to not kick out when that hobble strap is put on. We only had a handful of camels that had the barest training, the rest were flighty and volatile and while I had gained so much confidence handling some of our camels, the wilder ones still challenged me. I was grateful Gill was the one carefully, gently, soothingly putting on their foot straps and ducking well anticipated kicks from those less handled as they got used to this new routine.

There were certainly a few camels that responded better to my gentleness than Gill's brusquer manner. Jumuna was more likely to allow herself to be led if I was there with her, gently coaxing her on. Another camel that had come to us from a woman that loved him dearly but was no longer able to keep him was Rockhole. He was highly strung and very sensitive and often very flighty with Gill, but he behaved very well with me. Most of the older camels were easy for me to be around - it was the younger and friskier camels that constantly tested to see if they could find my boundaries and we had a lot of youngsters in our herd.

Our plan had been to have practice runs in the wagon around our paddock every single day, but time was slipping away from us and we'd only managed to do it once. This practice run had done nothing to soothe my worry over tackling *the* road.

We had put Jianti and Kunkaa in harness closest to the wagon. They were our first camels, who had arrived in our lives as babes and were now fully grown. In front of them were Andaria and Nev but despite giving them the command to walk up, none of the camels would budge. Gill put on his stern voice and they still wouldn't move. We'd come to trust Andaria completely and we were trying to figure out what was going on when Gill had an idea. He wanted to try putting Zu in harness in the lead, which appeared as a crazy idea. He'd had no training and wouldn't know what to do, but Gill was adamant he wanted to try him.

When I first saw Zu in amongst hundreds of other camels he'd stood so much taller than all the rest and in my imagination, in the days that followed he acquired the status of a mythical beast. I hadn't been wrong.

Gill slipped a rope around Zu's neck, all the time explaining to him what he wanted him to do. Then he led our gentle white giant to the head of the camels, slipped a harness with total ease over his head for the very first time and gently tapped him on the behind to get him to swing his bum around so he was in position for his harness to be clipped into place. Zu did everything as if he'd done it a million times before. This time when Gill called out 'walk up', Zu with one huge heave ho lurched the wagon forward and all our camels took off, all flowing as one, pulling our wagon. They'd wanted their king in the lead.

This was cause for celebration. Gill and I were beaming with delight. It was happening! Even though we were towing our small wagon behind us that had been transformed from an old car trailer and added extra weight, our big wagon rolled along the rutted track with ease. Zu pushed into his harness like an old timer. Our team of camels were all working together and so enthused by their own efforts, they began to cavort a little with excitement and pick up the speed. At first, we were all trundling along at a gentle trot. Gill was out in the front leading Zu and I could see him comfortably jogging along to keep up. Then the pace picked up even more and Gill was running even faster while yelling over his shoulder at me to put on the brake. I was and it wasn't slowing us down *at all* and without it, we were heading for a crisis. The camels had built up such a momentum that it wasn't possible to stop without a five-tonne wagon ramming them all up the bum. We desperately needed that brake. Over the rattle of the wagon pounding over the bumps and everything inside shaking and clanking and the stomping feet of the camels I could hear Gill yelling with all his might for me to put the brake on.

I was screaming so he could hear me, "It's not working, it's not working!" but he was so focused on staying ahead of the camels and not tripping and falling under their feet, he didn't hear me.

I had to find a way to stop the wagon and I had to do it FAST. I could only think of one option and I didn't know if I could pull it off, but I had no time to even think it through or even wobble in fear. I threw myself from our now galloping wagon and landed, rolling in the dirt, scratched and bruised but up on my feet at the speed of light and was now running alongside our small wagon. I was trying to find a handhold so I could pull myself in and not fall under its fast-moving wheels.

When I finally hoisted myself up into the wagon, nothing was as I'd anticipated. Sitting on top of the brake were camel saddles that were so damn heavy one almost needed a crane to lift them. Why anyone used such heavy saddles I had no idea but we'd purchased them in our early days of camels, thinking they'd be good to have. I could barely lift them on a strong day. There was no way I could move them further back into the wagon. I had one option. Using my feet as leverage, I hoisted the damn things overboard and freed up the brake, finally able to bring our runaway caboodle to a gentle halt.

Gill and I ran to each other and hugged as if we'd had a near death experience, so grateful that neither of us had been hurt. Then we collapsed on the ground too knackered to move. I was still gasping for air, covered in dirt and prickles and twigs. There was a trail of buckled saddles and their appendages on the track behind us and Gill was beside me on his knees, breathless and dripping with sweat. We took one look at each other and that was it, we couldn't stop laughing.

When Gill saw me jump from the wagon he'd thought I was baling out and had not expected me to turn into super woman on a rescue mission. I confess, I strutted around a little cockily while Gill sang praise for his amazing woman, the heroine of the day!

And while I was buoyed up with my own capability and soaking up all the praise, especially when the saga reached our friends and they all looked at me in awe and treated me like a supernova, the whole incident had done *nothing* to ease my fears about *the* fucking road.

The clock was ticking. Our lease ran out in a week and we would be leaving, ready or not - but before then we held a huge farewell party for all our friends and even Gill's beautiful mum Helen, who lived in Sydney had come.

It began just before sunset when the sky was magenta, streaked and rippled with gold. I had been worried there would not be enough food. I'd been so busy with so many last-minute preparations for leaving and I had not found time to even prepare one dish - yet our huge trestle table was laden with delicious food to eat. There were three huge fires burning to stave off the cold and I hadn't even had to gather wood. Friends had done it all for us. I stood basking in the firelight, brimming over with gratitude for all the lovely people that had come laden with gifts and food to share and chatting with our friends who all wondered where Gill could be, and where our wagon was.

This night was the big unveiling of our completed wagon and when I heard the light tinkling of camel bells I knew Gill and the wagon weren't far away. He appeared out of the bush like a scene from a fairytale and I held my breath in awe and wonder just like everyone else. In the last rays of sunlight our beautiful hand painted ark-like wagon appeared, garlanded in fairy lights. Gill was sitting up in the driver's seat as Jianti and Andaria nonchalantly pulled the wagon along the bush track that led to our camp with its tethered goats, honking donkey, dogs barking and a party full of people all waving and happy and here to celebrate with us and say goodbye.

Gill unharnessed the camels and led them off to feed and everyone crowded round our wagon, climbing in to see our queen size bed with its camel bed spread and big orange cushions and our funky pot belly stove. The stereo was playing and when one of our friends climbed down from the wagon, with a big smile on her face, she said, "Gee guys, whatever you do you certainly do it in style!" I had to laugh when another friend heard the doves cooing softly from their flowery painted home with their heart shaped windows, and going to check them out exclaimed loudly, "My God, this trip is almost becoming biblical!"

I have never really been one for parties. I have always preferred small groups of people to a crowd, to talk more intimately with a few rather than chat to many, but our party that blossomed under a sky full of stars was everything I hoped it would be. I was surrounded by people I loved, I was hugged and held and validated for what we had achieved and the vision we had held on to constantly through all the highs and lows. We had been disheartened many times. We'd had a house we thought we would never sell and days too numerous to count where we felt like naive fools with a dream that would never come together however hard we worked. We had been weary and worn out too many times to recall and yet together we had carried on, crossing every hurdle on our path, and we had made it - past all the letting goes as we lightened our load and said goodbye to our home, on past the building of a dream and all the preparation involved in making our vision a reality.

We hadn't even started on our adventure, but we were almost ready to embark upon it. I should have been excited and to a certain extent I was but standing there amongst so many friends, all giving and warm and sparkly and bright, whose presence made the summers bearable and warmed all our frosty days, I felt so sad. Would we ever find another place, another town to live in with such kind-hearted people that made my heart sing, that inspired me to be the best I could be and were happy when we shone?

This little town in the middle of the desert, 500 kilometres north or south from its nearest neighbour and much further east or west across the rugged desert, held much that I held dear. I had travelled a lot around Australia and I had never lived anywhere that had touched me so deeply. I did not know if any place we chose to live would ever come close to what we were about to leave behind. We wanted to move east not only because there were large blocks of land with rivers and mountains at a price we could afford, but because family and old friends lived nearby and the coast, oh what joy, would only be a few hours away.

After six years of living in the desert change was certainly calling but letting go of these people I knew and this town that I loved, with its suffering summers and its freakish dust storms that rumbled in unchallenged in a mountainous cloud of red grit, flocks of black cockatoos screeching across the sky and sitting under trees full of budgerigars in a chirping frenzy, nesting in the ancient gums of the dry river bed, letting go?

I am not sure I ever would.

Fifteen

The Love of Mother Mary

Two days before our departure, something totally unexpected happened.

I'd risen early and gone for a walk. It was freezing cold and each step I took crunched through frozen grass. We'd had some welcome torrential rain and everywhere I looked, strong green shoots were bursting from the frosty ground. I had a favourite place I was heading for under some big old trees where the ground was covered in purple flowers.

I couldn't shed my feeling of dread. Whatever I did, it was always there. It had haunted me for weeks and as we'd gotten closer to leaving I was even more exhausted from lack of sleep due to my worry.

I loved living in our camel paddock. If we could have stayed in there I may have settled down and never moved but because it was part of the airport buffer zone, they had a rule that no hard-hoofed animals could be there. They'd given us permission to have Bella and the goats but only because it was temporary.

I was sitting on the trunk of a huge fallen tree, revelling in the colours of the rosy dawn sky and the icy spiders webs that garlanded the bushes, sparkling in the pink light. All of a sudden, I had a revelation. It hit me like a bolt of lightning and in that moment, all my stress drained away. I felt totally clear and calm and I knew I was being shown another way. I hadn't realised until that moment how we can be so fixated on doing something a certain way, we block off other more suitable possibilities. The cause of all my anxiety had never been the road - it had been my focus on a certain direction which had disconnected me from my flow.

When I arrived back at camp Gill was up trying to light a fire with wood that was damp with frost. It smoked for a while before bursting into flames and reflected perfectly the conversation I was about to have. With cuppas in our gloved hands and shivering a little over the flames, I told Gill what had happened to me in the paddock. He looked shocked. He sat for a while in silence absorbing my words. I sometimes wished he'd gush a little but that's just not my Gill. He's not one to speak before he's thought it through which can challenge a little if you're as jumping up and down with excitement as I was.

We were a day away from leaving and for two years we'd nurtured a goal to travel east. As I'd sat on that log, I was shown a dirt track away from town that was peaceful and calm, quiet and serene and travelled for 500 kilometres before it reached its first very small town. It was the old disused service road that ran alongside the now abandoned old Ghan railway line and this track began about a kilometre away from our camel paddock gate. There was one massive obstacle if we were fixed on our course. This track headed south, not east - and the only reason I was embracing it wholeheartedly was because it felt absolutely, incredibly right. I lit up from within at the thought of it and I was certain Gill would feel that too, even though he was taking his time!

When he did speak, his concern was not about the drastic change in our direction. He seemed to be completely fine with that but he wanted to point out that while this alternative route would avoid all the hazards of speeding traffic and dangerous roads, it went right through the heart of wild camel country and we were bound to meet more bull camels. Wild bull camels felt like puppy dogs to me after contemplating for months head on collisions with speeding vehicles or slipping off the edge of treacherous roads and us all plunging to our deaths. Bring on the wild bulls, we could cope. "We'll terrify them," I told Gill laughingly, "You know how scary I can be when I'm mad!"

Then just like that smoking fire before it burst into flames, Gill looked at me with a huge grin and said, "OK, let's do it but I need to buy one more thing. If we are heading into bull camel country I want a cattle prod as well."

In that very moment of aligning with our true direction, Gill was hearing exactly what he needed to purchase for our new path and whatever challenges that may bring. That blessed cattle prod, an implement we would never *ever* usually have or use on any animal, in a crisis situation would prove to be our godsend.

I felt light and happy as we finished organising our wagon, ready for *the* big GINORMOUS day ahead. We had a few easily accessible containers with a mixture of all our food for daily use and lots of big drums full of rice, lentils, sultanas, nuts, sacks of potatoes, onions, pumpkins and hundreds of kilos of dried dog food, with even more sacks of chicken and parrot food. It was so rewarding when it was all packed and I had a satisfying feeling knowing that whatever happened, whatever other challenges we may face, at least we wouldn't starve.

All day we'd had one eye on the road that led to the airport. This was the road we'd exit on and we wanted to see if we could gauge the quietest time of day. It was only a kilometre that we had to travel along it, but it was busy with buses and trucks, coaches and taxis all coming and going to the airport and did not seem to pause even for a breath. I was certainly relieved to know that a few friends would be turning up at dawn to help us on our way.

We hadn't managed a single practice run with *all* the animals. We had no idea how long it was going to take to get every animal in place before we'd be ready for the road. We'd be towing the small wagon behind us where the goats would ride but we hadn't even practised getting them into it.

I was relieved that our dear rooster The Colonel and all his girls had finally managed to navigate the ladder into their new home and now went in and out with ease. We'd begun by putting bales of hay each side, so it had been easier for them to jump up and get in. Gradually we'd taken all the props away until all that was left was the ladder and by that time, their little haven between the wagon's wheels was home and they shimmied up those steps.

The dogs would be riding in the wagon and when they came out it would be on a lead. One of the biggest drawbacks about travelling through the outback with dogs was that more often than not the country was sprinkled with 1080 baits. Years before, in Western Australia, I'd lost my dearest friend Sprouty to a bait and it was an experience that had haunted me. It broke my fucking heart. For years if I even tried to speak of it I became a blubbering emotional mess. It is so inhumane, it is evil and yes, my concern over the welfare of my dogs was utmost. That's why they would *always* be on a lead and when we made camp, they would be on a chain. It was just how we had to do it if we wanted to keep them all safe.

We had six dogs coming with us including Patchy and Chia who were brother and sister, both rescued when they were a day old and hand reared by us. Though they were from a litter of huge pig hunting dogs, Patchy was a big dopey affectionate and guileless dog and huge like his parents, while Chia was like a little mouse in this litter of huge dogs. When we found Patchy he was being eaten alive by maggots and we'd nursed this sorry pup with his big sad eyes, back to life and onto vigour.

Chia looked like she'd been bred by a hyena. She was the oddest little dog we'd ever seen but she was the centre of our lives. She had been the tiniest, baldest, weakest little day old pup when we found her in the rainforest where her mother had taken her to die. For weeks she had trembled and dithered on the edge of life and every breath we thought would be her last. Then one day, she woke up and began seizing life by the balls. Chia lived for joy and everything she did was done with undiluted passion. She rarely swam in the ocean but when she did she swam so far out, onlookers would be freaking out on the beach with us as we all yelled and screamed at her to come back. I was freaked out she'd be gobbled by a shark or taken by a pelican. None of us were brave enough to swim out that far. It took her over a year to grow hair and when it came it was like a king tide - it tufted out between her toes, sprouted from her ears and grew thick down her back, but it never quite reached the end of her tail.

Another hairy specimen coming on the adventure was our black and grey wolfhound cross, Wunjo. I'd had her long before I met Gill and while she was generally placid, she didn't take any shit. She always looked out for me and could see right through veneers. People always found her uncomfortable. In all the years we'd been together, twice she'd snarled, growled and curled her lip and looked like some demented zombie because someone she didn't like had come too close to me. I hadn't seen what she had, but I knew my dog well enough to trust her. When we'd lived in the tropics and I went everywhere barefoot, several times she'd alerted me with a growl to snakes hiding in the grass, saving me from stepping on them and getting bitten.

She was so scruffy and wild looking and even though we tried to cut her toenails, she put up such a fight that they often grew so long they looked like talons. Wunjo was no ordinary dog. A shapeshifter, a witch, a wise beast indeed. Gill and I both recall our horror when out for a walk climbing high in the rainforest, following a river upstream and getting above its waterfall, we suddenly saw Wunjo slip from the bank and into the fast moving water before it went over the edge of the fall. I'd collapsed to my knees feeling sick. The water was full of rocks below and it would be a miracle if she survived. Gill was about to leap over boulders and make his way down the fall when we turned around and saw Wunjo standing behind us. We'd both seen her fall in the water and go over the edge the minute before, and yet she wasn't even wet. Life with this dog was full of weird and inexplicable events.

Then we had my faithful Moby who'd chased my car on a call into the local animal rescue, and two other young dogs Jypy and Squinty, who were still finding their place in our tribe and had yet to unveil some good stories.

Mr Bloss and Snowdrop were our two doves. Mr Bloss was a dapper little bird who looked as if he should have a fob watch and a waistcoat. Each day he would perch on his little verandah, looking around as if he had work to do and was about to fly off to some ministerial position, while snowdrop looked like she'd flown out of the pages of a fairy-tale. While their pretty little home under the eaves of our wagon was a little girlie for Mr Bloss, it suited Snowdrop perfectly.

Swinging along on one side in the front, right next to our comfortable seats and in the midst of all the action, were Beautiful and Charlie - our two corellas who'd been rescued from 22 years in a tiny aviary. These two had lived for the last two years in a giant aviary we'd built down one side of our house and even though they were now in a cage, they were loving all the attention. On the opposite side of the wagon was Jo, ready and eager to go.

The biggest challenge we faced was working out where all the camels would go and how to easily get the goats into their wagon, but once we got on that old Ghan line we had 500 kilometres of dirt road to work it all out. Hopefully by the time we reached civilisation, even if that was only a teensy little outback town, we'd have some semblance of flowing happily and harmoniously together.

I actually felt more emotion leaving the paddock behind than I had our home. I'd felt happier living simply out in the bush without neighbours and all their noise. And I loved having all our camels close.

One night when the moon rose full in the sky, Gill and I had laid in bed and watched our camels for hours. They were stomping up the dust, prancing silhouettes in silvery blue light and all the girls had been flirting with our majestic Zu who looked luminous in the moonlight, as if he'd flown down from the stars. The girls were all enticing him, flirting and frisking around their king then running wildly, kicking up the dust. We had watched this seductive dance, hiding in the darkness of our wagon and feeling a little like peeping toms.

But Gill and I had both agreed that while we would train our camels and work together with them, we never *ever* wanted to cull their wild spirits. We wanted them to always have time when they could be wild and free. We knew people who expected their camels to sit the second they gave the command. There's a difference when you ask them to 'hoosh' down and they have time to do so comfortably, without fear, in friendship and harmony and because they respect you - not because their noses are pegged and you'll pull on their line and hurt them, or they know they'll be punished for taking a second too long. Never ever did we want that. Let them shuffle for a moment if they needed to, let there always be room to breathe and always, let our relationship with *all* our animals be kind.

As the sun set for the last time on a world that felt safe, we went to move our tethered camels to fresh grazing. We wanted them all to have full bellies when we left in the morning. We both felt tired and vulnerable and finally, when all the camels had been done, we wearily walked back to our wagon. I was thinking of the words of a friend who had many camels and I'd told him at least we have five that are trained. He'd laughed and replied, "My love you only have one, Andaria!" and I knew what he said was true. I often buoyed up my confidence with a reassuring *at least we have five camels that are trained*, but what I failed to acknowledge was that four of those camels had pulled the wagon for less than an hour. That ain't trained!

You'd be foolish to not question yourself when you take on such an outrageous adventure, especially because so many animals were involved. We owed it to them to be sure we could do it. I always wanted to believe in the impossible, a world with no limitations. If you set your focus on doing something and believe in yourself, it can be done. I wanted to believe that was true, but had we dreamt way too big this time?

We wouldn't know until we tried and we'd gotten this far only because we thought we could. But in that fragile fleeting moment when everything that was safe and secure was slipping away too fast, I was full of self-doubt again. *What if, what if, what if! What if we fuck up, we don't even have a home to return to. What if we don't even make it five kilometres down the road?*

Our camel paddock was not a place that many people went to. Occasionally we'd come across an old spam tin with the lid peeled back from some long-ago bushman's camp, but that was it. Yet suddenly, Gill's attention was caught by something buried in the ground and he bent down and began scraping away the earth, uncovering a little statue of Mother Mary.

Neither of us is religious in the organised sense, but I have to bow my head in awe at the constant miracles of life that make up each new day. A tiny frog that sleeps for years in the sun-dried mud of the land, breaking free from its baked clay cask at the first patter of falling rain. The way a tiny crocus, so fragile and gold can burst into life despite the settling snow. The brightness of a full moon and its fingers of silvery blue light. Or the beauty of a blossomed rose, rich and red and dripping with the rain.

I can't clutch what I know to be holy and I shy away from naming it, but I do feel a force that flows through me and guides me when I am true to what feels right for me, and honour who I am. When I surrender instead of resist, release rather than hold on, and always when I choose joy rather than money.

This little Mother Mary statue, all imitation cream ivory and carved from a mould, gave me a feeling that chirruped inside and had me shouting,

"Yes, yes, yes! We can do it, we can do it! I know we can do it!"

We sat around our fire that night feeling so full on the goodness of our life, eating our last supper that was cooked by dear friends who bought *everything* with them so we didn't have to get up from our chairs once. They brought the food, the plates, the cups and cutlery and even the wine. I was so grateful to be able to sit and for one night at least, do *nothing*. Such a simple little luxury that our friends had given us, and yet it was the greatest gift.

We sat until late, savouring what was certain in our lives, holding onto the last embers of the night to ward off the approaching day.

Excited, yet scared shitless.

Sixteen

Finally

We rose so early the following day that I felt like I'd barely slept. It was still dark and freezing cold and after rugging up, we lit a big fire and put the billy on. We had a huge day ahead and expected our friends to arrive with the dawn. They were going to help us launch our wagon and we wanted to be as prepared for their arrival as we could.

I wished I was Chia, snuggled up sleeping in our warm bed, instead of shaking with cold and with butterflies in my belly that felt as if they wearing steel capped boots. What we were about to do was scary. People think when you go on big adventures you're always brave, but being brave for me was also being ok with feeling afraid. That passing fear, even though it was a regular visitor and loved to leave me quaking, was not going to stop me from doing what I knew we could do. I was afraid and brave, quaking and strong all at the same time.

We were beginning a routine that would be whittled and changed, buffed and perfected with each kilometre we travelled but on that first day, our animals were all over the place. Everything was all trial and error and we made so many lengthy mistakes that organising all the animals took hours. Our wilder camels were belligerent and refused to move and we were both struggling to stay calm.

It would have all been so much easier if we'd pegged our camels noses and as we coaxed, coerced and finally heaved and dragged wild camels to our wagon, there were many moments when we'd wished we had. I'm grateful that every time I thought this, it was fleeting. This all *had* to get better. It just *had* to. My compassion was my compass, my dream of working together in a more conscious way with these animals was at the forefront of this challenge but in those early days, there were many moments we were pushed to extremes and found ourselves wishing we'd chosen an easier way.

We even put on some relaxing music, thinking it would calm us all down and relax and soothe our more resistant critters but it did nothing to help the situation at all. Our friends were filming our early morning preparation for launch and all that changed was that we were now on film, cursing and swearing loudly as we dragged kicking camels who were determined to head in the opposite direction, towards the wagon to a bizarre background of chanting Buddhist monks or the floating melodies of the pan pipes. It was all just slightly incongruous.

We had five camels in the front, pulling the wagon. Two sets of two across and then Zu, our bull, in the middle and in the lead. The other camels were tied from the back of the wagon in strings of two or three. We had no idea if this formation was going to work, it was just a matter of trying it out and seeing for ourselves.

One of the many reasons I love camels so much is because they are such characters, especially Lady Caroline. As stately and as dignified as she liked to be, she was a funny bod - she had all these little ways she liked to do things and with us she had the freedom to be herself. We were all working together and we had to find harmonious ways that felt good for all of us! But finding *her way* often took time, and it took hours to discover that she liked to approach being harnessed from the rear of the wagon as she was led by Gill. She appreciated little pauses as she was led alongside the wagon, to survey the other camels and have a look around. When we honoured this process, she was perfectly happy to step into harness behind Zu. If we tried to speed it up we were met with resistance and the entire process took longer. There was no rushing her. We'd carefully decided to put her behind Zu in the team. Just like her relationship with Gill, she looked at Zu as her equal which was very different from how she saw little plebeian me. Even though I received more regular acknowledging sniffs, I was still a long way down in the pecking order.

There were many little foibles like this that we had to deal with, but the regal parade that Lady Caroline did enroute to being harnessed was set in place from day one and it never changed. This camel embodied being a queen and I knew I had a lot to learn from her.

Our efforts the day before to monitor the traffic on the road had been pretty pointless. Even if we had discovered a quiet time, we were in no position to make deadlines. We were leaving when we were ready and by the time we finally got everyone in place, it was well past lunch. If we'd left any later it would have almost been time for bed. We only had a few hours of sunlight left.

I felt as if everything began to move in slow motion as the wagon finally began to move, bouncing over the ruts as it headed towards the gate, where if the clodhopping butterflies in my stomach didn't stop, I may have to break for a spew. There was no turning back now, no safety nets to catch us if we fell and no safe havens to slink to with our tails between our legs. Failure was not an option.

As we walked, I soaked up and lingered on the familiarity of everything we knew that we had come to love. The disappearing eucalyptus tree we'd camped under, sewn up dog coats under, washed our dirty dishes under, sat drinking wine with friends under and in our last week of residence had had millions of black hairy caterpillars dropping on us from its shady boughs that we were constantly rescuing from drowning in the dog's water or the bath. That lovely tree, so full of memories, the silent onlooker of so much treasured time was getting further and further away, fading already into my past.

The two camels in the paddock next door were running alongside the fence with us, keen to come on our adventure. Our friend Wayne who'd been the knight in shining amour that bought Munki to us was up there, filling up their giant baths with water and he stood waving goodbye, getting smaller as we got closer to the gate then he too, so familiar and safe, faded away.

Green, green, green footsteps moving through green and lush. Tufts of buffle grass bursting with life and vigour after the rain. There were yellow flowers growing everywhere, so tiny - like fairy's flowers, too tiny to see their exquisite beauty unless you got up close. After years of aching to leave on this adventure, I felt like a condemned man walking to the hangman's noose as I walked that kilometre to the gate. Time had slowed and everything had become so vivid. Could we turn back? Was it too late? It was a half-hearted call and I knew it.

I was walking beside the wagon when we reached the gate. My job was to slow the traffic and make sure the animals were all OK. One of our friends was riding in the wagon controlling the brake, with Gill leading us all out in front of Zu. Another friend drove slowly behind us, slowing the traffic. How grateful we were for our friends.

We went through that gate, cockies in cages swinging from side to side, screeching wildly. The dogs all barked with excitement, while our camels kicked out and bucked as we ploughed over tufts of grass and mounded earth and finally, after years of planning, made it onto the road. The traffic did not show us any mercy and when I stepped out into the road to slow a fast approaching car, he gave me the finger as he hurtled past.

After our blessings from Mother Mary and our initiation with the eagles, after all our dreams of working with our animals in a more conscious way, I yelled after him, "You fucking arsehole!" I could not believe it. We'd barely been on the road for five minutes and I had been given the finger and sworn like I never do *and* at a complete stranger. When

I managed to grab a moment with Gill, he told me he'd sworn at someone too! We had to laugh. It was love and light all the way with us!

We careered along that roadside trying to avoid wiping out young saplings, as we tucked ourselves as far off the road as we could to let busses full of tourists waving madly and their windows crammed with cameras past. There were cars doing emergency stops and people jumping out of their vehicles with video recorders, careless of whether they blocked the road as they rushed from their cars to film a sight never seen on the road before as Gill and I, bold dreamers that we were, launched nervously into our dream.

Shaking but happy we left that frantic pace behind, turning onto the road heading south. Just another 500 metres, a few more cars of tourists and our dirt track would begin. Sitting under a tree was a hitch hiker with a big Mexican hat, strumming on his guitar as he waited for a lift {Gill swears he didn't have a Mexican hat, but that's what I saw}. His mouth fell open, his guitar playing all forgotten when he saw us coming towards him. I saw him shake his head from side to side and rub at his eyes. Had he had too much sun? Was he in the throes of some crazy hallucination? When he looked again blinkingly and realized we were for real, his face cracked into the biggest grin and still shaking his head he said, "Bloody Hell, I never thought I would ever see anything like this!"

We passed him with a wave, breathless and excited with our noisy parrots still squawking and the dogs still adding to the ruckus erupting from our wagon that was bouncing along merrily in the faded ruts of the road. We could see the old Ghan line just a stone's throw away, the red sand of the track dappled with the orange glow of the fading light and the sky a wash of purple, pinks and gold.

Our camp that night was not far away from the embers of the night before and the fire we'd shared on our last night with a home. It had taken us all day to travel a kilometre but we were radiant we'd done that and we were both shaking and rippling with excitement as we hugged one another. There are no words for moments like this, we were both just riding the sensations, waves of feeling crashing on the shore. The culmination of so much work was about to unfold. We had finally broken free and the future stretched for thousands of kilometres ahead of us, right through the heart of wild bull camel country, through land that was rugged and bleak. We had no idea what tomorrow would bring but we stood eagerly on the edge of the unknown.

Seventeen

Down the Red Sandy Track

We didn't make it far that first night. The light was fading fast and we decided to pull up and make camp. It had been a long and hard day and now, at the end of it, there was still so much to do before we could sit down. The chickens, parrots, pigeons and dogs all had to be watered and fed. Goats needed to be let out and watered and camels had to be unharnessed and have their hobble straps done up around their ankles, then tethered out for a feed.

Gill was handling all the wilder camels and I found it *very* stressful. I'd be holding their heads and trying to keep them calm while Gill would be carefully squatting, just out of reach of their feet, slapping their ankles gently with a rope until they stopped reacting with a kick. Only then could he get in closer, but he was always so attentive to their every move as he buckled up that hobble strap and always ready to move fast if he had too. If he watched them, he could anticipate a kick by the way they shifted their weight from one foot to another. One moment of inattention and one well-placed kick and the whole show would be over.

While it was fraught with peril for Gill handling the wilder camels, even handling a quiet one could be dangerous if we were not paying attention. Gill was always warning me to stay focused when tying knots in the camels ropes. You could lose a limb if you let your finger get caught in a knot and the camel bolted during the process. Everything we did with them needed our undivided attention and it was such a relief when we'd tethered them all out and could finally succumb to our exhaustion. There was so much lush feed growing and they were all soon contentedly feeding. They were always happy when their bellies were full.

By the time we collapsed into our fancy faux fur camping chairs Gill and I didn't even have the energy to light the fire and get warm, let alone negotiate the big heave ho required to climb into our wagon and fall into bed.

We just sat there shivering with cold, in the dark, sighing and gasping with incredulity that we'd *done* it. Our one little kilometre of bold and brave travel had catapulted us into a reality we'd mapped, plotted, planned and mulled over for almost two years. Yet as tired as I was I didn't even know if I would sleep that night. I'd felt brave about the bull camels when we were safely tucked in our paddock with a lovely fence around us. Now we had nothing to protect us from them - only ourselves and our ingenuity and I prayed that would be enough.

Fears are such funny little things, they sprout a little like mushrooms. You pluck out one and another, sometimes a crop, pops up in its place. My fear over the road from hell had been replaced with a fresh worry that wild bulls would come marauding while we slept. I was so tired and I often slept really deeply. What if I didn't wake up? What if our animals needed help in the night? Should we sleep with the cattle prod in the bed beside us and the shot gun loaded ready to fire, or was I being paranoid? Gill didn't know either, but he reckoned we'd be safe for now. After all, we were sitting within sight of the twinkling lights of Alice's little airport and we were still on the outskirts of town. It was a fair bet that these menacing bulls would be roaming in the wilder places. At least that's what we hoped.

We slept anyway, so deeply that the following morning we woke up with a start. The sun was already filling our wagon with its rays of golden light. We had intended to rise before the dawn and get an earlier start on the day, but it was past lunchtime when we were finally ready to call 'walk up' and get the wagon rolling down that red dirt track.

I have always been an animal lover but that morning I did not even like my goats. Those horrid creatures had us running around for hours. They'd teasingly jump onto the back ledge of their wagon - the one we were *desperate* to get them into and then they'd leap off, legs kicking out, cavorting and playing and running away from us before circling back and looking as if they were about to oblige us. Having us sighing with relief that they were almost in the wagon, off they'd frolic again. The rotters were having so much fun at our expense. By the time we had caught them all and bundled them into their little wagon that was all cosy and full of edible branches for them to eat on the trip, I was near to tears and more than ready to get moving.

As we slowly set off, leaving the airport behind with its quiet rumble of little planes landing or taking off and turning our backs on the fading reds and oranges of the ruggedly beautiful MacDonnell ranges, I was sad and happy all at the same time. Sad to be leaving so much I loved but so happy to finally be living a life where *everything* was unknown.

The colour of the track was a rich terracotta and on each side grew saltbush, fresh and plumped up from the recent rains. In amongst its sage green leaves were clumps of succulent pig weed, a plant that was so nutritious we often ate it and it was one of the foods that had helped Munki to thrive. It had pretty little pink flowers like tiny sun jewels. There were bushes of wild tobacco covered in purple star flowers with rough hairy leaves and another fantastic plant for helping animals put on condition - precious ruby dock.

Since having camels I'd found it impossible to just enjoy the bounty of the bush without evaluating its culinary potential for our herd and everywhere I looked, the earth was covered in wild flowers of every colour. The country spoke of abundance and feast and we couldn't have left at a better time.

As Gill walked in front leading the camels with Bella walking close beside him, I sat in the driver's seat of the wagon riding the brake. There were definitely nerves, how could there not be with all these animals to keep safe and well and with help getting further away with each step, but we were finally on the road and I couldn't believe it.

The camels were walking peacefully along, the only sounds the soft muted melody of the handcrafted bells they wore around their necks, the creaks of the wagon as she groaned over the bumps in the rough old dirt track and an occasional shriek from our excited corellas, as they reached out from the wagon and grabbed mouthfuls of leaves from the trees that grew close to the track as we followed the Old Ghan line on our way to who knows where.

Ideally, we'd hoped to have left much earlier in winter and our only concern about our daily progress was that we could not travel in the heat of summer. It would be too hot for us and our animals and while we didn't want to rush and miss out on enjoying our journey, we needed to maintain a steady pace and cover a good distance while the weather was still reasonably cool.

For Gill, watching the wagon rolling along after two years of building it was a momentous occasion. His concerns were so different from mine and focused on keeping everything flowing. Were all his welds holding up? Had he made the wagon too heavy? He walked up and down, checking everything. How were the camels harnesses fitting, did any look loose or likely to rub? How were the camels working together? Were they all comfortable in their positions? Gill's facial expression was creased in deep thought and I couldn't tell if everything was OK. When he came back around my side I managed to ask him how he felt. With a big grin he affirmed, "Exhilarated!"

It was only when we pulled up for a break to let the dogs out for a pee and check everyone was ok that he laughingly told me he'd felt like Noah must have done when the floods finally came. The ark all loaded up with animals bellowing, squawking and barking, watching his cynical neighbours getting washed away as he finally got confirmation he hadn't just been a fool with crazy vision.

We hadn't had cynical neighbours but we'd had our cynics and who could blame them. When you are convinced your method is the only way, you're going to feel challenged by anyone challenging the status quo. If you didn't believe it was possible to handle camels *without* nose pegs or travel with so many different animals, of course you'd expect us to fail.

And while it was fantastically reassuring to be ambling along a beautiful red dirt track with a mellow wintry sun warming the chills of the day we were certainly not foolish enough to even think we'd come anywhere close to nailing it, but seeing everything flowing smoothly and the wagon doing its job lifted a lot of apprehension from both me and Gill.

The camels pulled the wagon as if they'd done it a million times before and I could slowly feel myself beginning to relax as we approached a small gully. It had dried out from the recent rain but still looked really boggy in the middle. Gill led the camels down the slope while I cranked on the brake. It didn't work as strongly as I'd hoped, but it slowed the wagon slightly as we made the descent. We were in such a flow with all the camels working together, when out of nowhere a group of trail bike riders came blatting along the track behind us and impatient to get ahead, suddenly veered through the bush around us making so much noise we all nearly jumped out of our skins. Birds flew startled from the trees and our scared camels went into a bolt that took us off the track and got our little wagon with the goats in it bogged in deep muddy ruts.

Gill started digging to see if he could free the wagon, but it wasn't going anywhere. We were well and truly stuck. The quad bikes had raced off on their noisy adventure and were long gone, their distant progress marked by the trails of dust that rose like smoke from a bush fire. We were just wondering what to do when we saw several 4WDs pull up nearby.

Though still dirt, the main road south meandered alongside the old Ghan line track that we were on, sometimes side by side, and at other times several kilometres away. At that early stage of our trip we didn't know this. The section of the track we had just travelled down meandered a far way inland from the road so we hadn't heard any vehicles. We felt as if we were walking through the middle of a desert and were already far away from the civilized life we had left behind, so it was a shock to see even more 4WDs pull up and people leaping from them eager to see what was happening.

I was mortified at the number of vehicles that had stopped. I prefer to work my problems out privately, but obviously my new life of being homeless and on the road didn't cater for that luxury. I found it all too much, being stuck in a boggy hole on the first day of our adventure and apparently, only a few kilometres down the track! Everything had been so labour intensive I felt as if we'd travelled much further.

As the crowds gathered around us documenting our failure in photographs and film, I wanted to slink away and pretend I had nothing to do with this outrageous spectacle that was stuck up to its axle in mud.

I'd heard from many people who'd travelled with camels how in your face the tourists could be. I didn't want to respond with anger or frustration in the same way others I knew had. We'd only just begun and while this aspect would on some days be almost overwhelming, what I realised as I stood in that group of curious and intrigued people was that they wanted to help us. They were not looking at our bogged wagon and seeing failure. They were looking at us with glowing admiration and genuinely wanted to help get us back on the track.

I found myself a little speechless as they began looking for ropes and backing in their 4WDs, even getting muddy to strap a tow rope on our wagon and with the grunt of a diesel engine, they towed her out of the bog. Everyone cheered, the dogs barked, the parrots shrieked. It was fantastic.

And while my first response had been to cringe and hide, as our rescue mission unfolded I couldn't help remembering all the times when I'd sat in meditation and heard the words *whenever you need help it will be there*. How miraculous it was that the two roads we were all travelling on had briefly merged at the very point we'd needed that help. Of course, people were going to film us. We were like a scene from a fairytale but most of all (and I had not anticipated this), our brief connection with these people had been so full of love. They'd felt what we were doing and while they may not have been able to explain or even define those feelings, we could see they were visibly moved.

Even our wild camels behaved like little angels and had stood patiently and calmly for the good hour we'd been held up on the side of the road. These passing strangers had been in rapture when we showed them our chickens sitting happily, clucking away like little old ladies in their bed of dried grass with wildflowers strewn in amongst them that we'd gathered along the way for them to eat. When we led everyone around to the doves and their pretty home and they saw their little faces peeping out from their heart shaped windows, they were speechless. Some were even choking back their tears. They had never seen anything like this before and had not expected to be moved so deeply as they travelled down a dusty outback road on their way to the next tourist attraction.

Looking at our life through their eyes was so empowering for me. It gave me so much confidence in what we were doing. They were our first cheerleaders and they hadn't thought we were crazy like I'd imagined they would. Instead, they'd admired us for living so bravely and with such trust. They even told us they wished they could be more like us and less afraid. These lovely people had helped us out of a bog and yet they were thanking us and telling us how grateful they were. I truly hadn't expected that. As they went to jump back in their 4WDs, one of the women yelled back, "We hope you find your dream, somewhere really beautiful to live - you certainly deserve it."

As we continued down the track, Bella our much loved but so stubborn donkey was walking alongside Gill, trying to suck on his shirt or nibble his hat and over the soft clanking of the camels bells and our wagon groaning like an old dame over the corrugations in the road, I could hear Gill muttering and mumbling at Bella, "Get off, leave me alone, stop it."

The soothing cacophony of our life on the road.

Eighteen
Tracks in the Sand

We pulled up that night in a fairytale scene. The ground was thick with wild flowers and there was a dried billabong surrounded by short knarly trees, their beautiful weeping branches cascading into the dried up waters that was now a bed of mud and reeds. We were riding on such a high, elated at our progress. Even unharnessing and handling our wilder camels had been so much easier. We sat around our camp fire after all the jobs had been done, feeling so content as we waited for our dinner to cook on the coals. The animals were all happy. The goats and camels were scoffing down mouthfuls of flowers and our dogs, all in blue jackets, were sleeping in the holes they had dug in the sand. To top it all off a fleeting visit from a friend had informed us that we'd travelled eight kilometres, and that was pretty good considering it was only our second day and we'd been stuck in a bog.

Later that night, when the moon rose like a huge silvery lantern casting its light on the camels that now sat sleeping on a crumpled bed of paper daisies and billy buttons, their breath steaming from the cold night air, I really couldn't see how life could get any better.

How differently the morning came about. We got up as the darkness gave way to the red glow of dawn like the coals of a fire burning softly on the horizon. It was so bitterly cold it howled in my bones. Nothing was going to make our early mornings easy. We both had to push ourselves through a forcefield of resistance just to get out of bed each day. The ground was covered with frost and the water in the dogs bowl was a solid block of ice. The only place for any sane person was back in bed, but if we wanted to move at all, any day, we *had* to start early.

We'd already worked out that the best use of time when we first got up was for me to focus on lighting the fire, boiling a billy of water for our cuppa and getting a big pot of porridge on to cook for breakfast. Gill would go and check on all our animals and move our camels to fresh feed so they'd have a few extra hours grazing before we left.

It was just getting light and we were about to sit down and have our cuppas when we heard a distant rumbling sound that appeared to be heading our way. We could feel the earth trembling and all the leaves on the trees began to quiver. Whatever was coming felt ominous. We stood anxiously, completely unable to respond because neither of us had any idea what was about to occur.

All of a sudden, a helicopter zoomed in and began circling really low above us. We were choking on dust, our camels were freaking out and I was terrified they'd hurt themselves by trying to run on their leg ropes. The goats that had all been grazing freely bolted as fast as they could and disappeared into the haze. I was waving my arms madly, trying to get the pilot to move off. He had to have seen the impact he was creating and yet he circled for a few times before flying off. I was so focused on the safety of our animals in that moment that it was an even bigger shock when we heard the sound of thousands of hard hoofs galloping, pounding the soft desert earth into dust just twenty metres away. Down the other side of the fence line came all the terrified cattle and on the tail of these mustered beasts were several motorbikes and after them the 4WDs revved past, gunning their engines madly, driving like maniacs barely visible in the billowing haze of dust.

When the hell had finally passed, we were left gasping for breath with our hearts beating madly, shaking our heads at the ugliness of modern-day mustering. It used to be such a gentle art.

I was so relieved when we found the frightened goats, panting but safe. I'd felt terrified that they'd cut under the fence and gotten in the way of the cattle. The camels had all settled down and no one had been hurt. It was such a brutal start to the day but even that passed like a bad dream and we were left, once again, ankle deep in flowers with the track looking like burnished gold and flocks of galahs sweeping down curiously to check us all out.

I love winter in the desert. It can be bitterly cold and yet the sun shines and the sky is usually always the brightest blue. There were no winter doldrums like I remembered from growing up in the UK, when life can turn bleak and grey for months on end.

I was feeling really happy about our sudden change of plan to head south instead of east, because we'd been told we'd travel through some stunning country. We had been so busy all the time we had lived in Alice that we hadn't even (shamefully I have to admit) travelled further than ten kilometres down this track. It was all new and I felt excited at what we would discover along the way.

My fears were definitely still there. They gave me a tightness in my stomach when I thought of bull camels and they made me double check everything.

Ropes weren't too long so that animals could trip and camels were able to walk easily besides one another, not being dragged. The parrots cages, sitting up the front near the driver's seat and hanging just slightly over the sides of the wagon, were securely tied in. I don't think fears are ever meant to fade completely, they're what keeps us on our toes and everything safe - but they are meant to be there in the background and for the first time since we left that's where they were.

We got on that road faster that day. It was still a lengthy process, but the goats had worn themselves out and had no fight when it came to loading them in their wagon and Ninny even jumped in all by herself. That was monumental progress! The camels were keen to go and when we finally called out that command to "Pull em up, come on pull em up" it was accompanied by the ritual shrill, eardrum-piercing squawk from our parrots and all six dogs howling with excitement, whilst the wagon surged forward in a powerful pull that soon had us up over the slight rise of the old train embankment and back on that red sandy track.

Everything was so new and for me, that initial launch of the wagon was often the most stressful time and trying to stay focused and attentive in all that noise was a challenge. We were a mad house on wheels but however much we tried, we were never able the entire trip to coerce, threaten or even bully our excited animals into silence during our morning launch.

We took it in turns to lead the camels. We wanted to get them all on reins eventually but until they got used to pulling the wagon, one of us was always in the front. I loved leading the camels, striding out, feeling fresh and alive, enjoying the chilly nip in the air. Looking out for lizards that always seemed to sun bathe in the openness of the track and shooing them like naughty kids home, and checking all the faded tracks of animals in the sand. Gill seemed to know what every track was and taught me how to spot the different animals. The snake-like weave of the lizard's tail with the tiny prints of his feet, criss-crossed with rabbit's, bird's and a tiny trail that wove in and out that could have been little marsupial mice. Occasionally my heart would do the biggest lurch at the huge heart-like print of a solitary camel, just a faint echo of a distant traveller who had also passed this way.

I could have walked for miles that day, but after only a few hours Gill noticed some wheel studs that needed fixing on the small wagon, and wanted to stop before they broke completely and we lost a wheel. We pulled up in a layby where every tree was encrusted in dirt. It was a ghoulie, godforsaken place and I didn't want to stay there long.

I couldn't help feeling frustrated. We'd only just begun to flow when we had to stop and fix something. At least we'd come well prepared for everything, and had a humongous and heavy generator/welder that lived under the raised platform that the goats sat on. To get to it though we had to unload the goats, brace our arm muscles to hoist it out and then lug it to where Gill needed to work. With all his tools in place, it didn't take him long to realise the job would take longer than he initially thought. Glum, I felt so glum. We couldn't have picked a worse place to stop.

Sometimes the only thing you can do is get on with the job at hand and make the most of it. I began to gather firewood and get the billy boiling for a cup of tea, while Gill started unharnessing the camels and leading them to the outer edge of our dustbowl for feed. I was glad he was handling them. Even some of our quieter camels could be dangerous and some would even try to barge straight over the top of us. In those early days I often fantasised about leaving the naughty ones behind and just dropping them off somewhere, never to be seen again. They pushed us beyond all our limits.

Old Jumuna was still likely to kick out if we didn't do everything really slowly. While we had made huge progress and transformed our initial relationship, we hadn't spent that much time with her after the shocking incident when she'd self-harmed because about a month later she had unexpectedly given birth. After the hell she'd already gone through we didn't want to create any stress for our new mum and had respectfully kept our distance, which meant that Jali was still wild at eight months old when we began to handle her. When Gill and I had initially seen Jumuna's calf freshly birthed into the world we'd gasped, kinda shocked. Usually baby camels are such pretty things but she was pug faced and fierce looking. Instead of long lanky legs, hers were short and thick. Everything about her was stout and she was *so* strong.

One of the craziest aspects of our adventure was having so many unhandled camels. Some kicked, others bolted, a few barged, but only crooked nosed Mozzee chose the path of least resistance. Do nothing at all. Refuse to move, dig your feet into the ground, close your eyes and pretend no-one is there. He'd gotten his name because of his mellow personality and I absolutely adored him, but when he did his statue impersonations when we were trying to get all the animals organised for the day ahead he could be so frustrating, but he wasn't alone in that! We were travelling with so many different personalities. Every animal had different needs, different fears, different issues, different likes and dislikes. Some camels didn't like others and others were only happy if they were walking next to their best friend, some camels liked to be in the front, others at the back.

Working it all out was like playing a game of chess in multiple dimensions with a galactic grandmaster. There was nothing simple about what we'd taken on and in those early days we were constantly rearranging and refining *everything*. Ourselves, the way we rose each day, the order we fed the animals, the order we unharnessed the camels, the timing of our morning cuppa. The tiniest little act could have far reaching consequences and we had to become bigger than we'd ever been, rise above it all, observe every little detail and not miss *anything*-. Every turn of the wagon's wheels, the slightest change of sounds, an unexpected creak, the strain of a harness, a look of distress, a flap of wings from a dove. It was with this hawk-eyed precision Gill had honed in on our loose wheel nut, a job we thought would be quick to fix but took two days.

The only blessing of this dusty abode were two gentle young men who came to our camp, shyly asking if it was alright to stop and say hello. They'd been brought up on aboriginal communities where their parents had worked as teachers, and from a young age had learned to hunt and find bush food. They both had a strong connection with the land and knew all the edible plants, and were on their way back to Alice after hunting with the tribe. As they were about to get into their battered little sedan, they offered me a container of witchety grubs and told me I could eat them raw and *alive*. I didn't want to shock their sensitivity with some lurid expletives but I was horrified. I had never seen these huge lily-white grubs before and they were beautiful. I have total respect for people that live from the land and gather their food but there was no way I was going to pop a little creature into my mouth and gobble it up. Time stood still as I stared in mute horror, frantically trying to find the right words to refuse what was being offered in such a kind and heartfelt way by our two oh so very polite guests and finally only managing,

"Oh, bloody hell, that's awful I couldn't.'

It was such a relief to be on our way in the morning. Our ghoulie camp had smothered us in dust. We had it caked in our hair, up our noses and as we harnessed our camels, we were coughing it up.

After an hour or two (one doesn't really know when one doesn't own a watch), we passed one of the old railway sidings now being run as a bit of a museum. We'd hoped to be able to fill up our water tanks and were disappointed to find it closed. We had only a little water left and would have to be really frugal until we reached the next tank. We had no choice but to continue along the sandy track that bordered the homestead's fence line.

The countryside was beginning to change - lots of deep red sandy dunes, desert oaks and large evergreen trees with broad drooping branches that were home to numerous nests of crows with their lazy and languid call. While it was a majestic landscape, a bush fire had recently blazed through and if there had been any ground cover it was now black and charred. The camels were looking around, horrified. Their bottom lips were quivering, their eyes bulging in dismay. The road we were on stretched for miles to the horizon, a ribbon of red weaving through a black sea. There was no food for the camels anywhere - they could see this and were beginning to grumble and moan. I certainly shared their concern. Life was not going to be happy for any of us if, at the end of the day, this lot didn't get a good feed.

We were all really sluggish. My own body ached and I could tell the camels were all struggling from their own lack of fitness. All the time we'd had them, we'd asked little from them and they'd come to see us as a source of pleasure. A good rub or a scratch, the deliverers of tasty morsels and culinary delights. We were all adjusting to the change in our relationship that now called for us all to work together.

The winter sun had been getting hotter by the day as summer began to take hold. My face felt reddened and my feet so sore. I hadn't walked so far for years and my own far from fit body was feeling the strain but there was still no feed and Gill wanted to push on. I was worried, it was getting late in the day. The sun was already dipping low and we would soon lose the light. All I wanted was to sit down and rest yet there was still so much to do and we hadn't even found a decent place to pull up and give our animals a feed.

We kept pushing on. Just a little further. This burnt out country couldn't last long, surely? Perhaps around that next bend we'd come to a great place to camp, or over that next rise, or perhaps a few more kilometres down the road. On and on we pushed, hopeful we'd soon leave the burnt out landscape behind.

It was ridiculous to carry on exhausted but it was in our blunders that we learnt and grew.

Nineteen

Wake Up Call

I was so exhausted I was struggling to put one foot in front of the other as we finally pulled off the track and came to a halt under a huge desert oak tree. The camels moods had not improved and they were really pissed off. They could see there was no food. They grumbled and moaned and kicked out as we rushed to unharness them in the fast fading light. I'd had so many moments when I cursed our soft-hearted idealism and the lack of nose pegs, and this was one of them. Nose pegs would have made our job of handling our camels so much easier, and safer too.

We'd kept pushing on *for* the camels. We'd done our best to find feed but there was nothing we could do to ease the dissent that crept through them all, making even those we thought trained hard to handle. I'd just unharnessed our chocolate brown diva Kunkaa and I should have known better. She was always fierier than Jianti, who she'd grown up with. As I was leading her towards a small bush to temporarily tether her while we tried to sort out the rest of our rioting camels, I failed to pay attention. I desperately needed to sit down and I was not focused on the job at hand. I couldn't wait to be relaxing by the fire with all the jobs done, drinking our last cold beer.

In the midst of my daydream, Kunkaa leapt into the air and as she did, her front foot clouted me full in the face with an almighty whack. I fell backwards onto the ground feeling so sick and dizzy. My face throbbed and fuck, I didn't want to be paranoid, but I had no idea if I was about to die. Had she fractured my skull? I lay flat on my back looking up at the sky, while everything became a faint echo as I wavered in and out of consciousness. Even Gill couldn't stop what he was doing to attend to me, though he managed to run over with ice from the fridge to put on my face, ordering me to stay still while he sorted out the camels.

I remember laying there for a while in a blur, completely unaware of what was unfolding around me. In Gill's urgency to reach me when he saw me go down, he had quickly tied Zu's rope to a small bush. When he finally got back to Zu he was laying with his head downhill, unable to get himself back upright because of the slope and was starting to choke on his cud. If Gill had been any longer with me we would have lost Zu, but I didn't know that until much later.

As the dizziness eased I sat up, periodically dropping my head between my legs as a wave of sickness passed. I didn't even know if I could stand upright and yet I *still* yearned to be sitting in that camp chair drinking that last beer, only now I was craving a cigarette and it'd been a long time since I'd been a smoker. In fact I wanted one so badly, I was even trying to work out how far away the road was and if there'd be the slightest likelihood of a passing car travelling down a remote dirt road and whether or not I'd look too freaky looming out of the darkness, looking like a wild dishevelled woman with my face all swollen and bruised, demanding cigarettes. Even in my bleary state it didn't take me long to conclude that I would.

I felt fiendish - I was *that* desperate for a smoke and if an angel of light had descended from the heavens right there and then and told me I had one wish, without a single hesitation I would have blown it on a fag.

I sat in the dirt waiting for Gill and when the chaos we called camel handling had passed, he came and led me to my camping chair, deeply worried that I'd been hurt. He sat me down and began examining my face, fingering along my cheekbone, checking for a break. When he was satisfied I was OK, he began collecting some kindling for a fire.

We were sitting by a fire pit that looked as if it had been used the night before. There were a few half-burnt logs still poking from the ashes and the remains looked pretty fresh. Gill built up the kindling with some dried leaves and was about to strike a match and light it up when he noticed a cigarette packet that had slipped down between two of the big rocks edging the fire pit.

Our mouths fell open in delight and bemusement when we saw it still had six cigarettes in it and six was the most perfect amount. After the hell Gill had just gone through as he'd tethered all our crazy bucking camels and fed and watered all our other animals too, then struggling to keep upright had briskly walked our dogs, all the time freaked out and worried about me, I was in no doubt he'd be puffing along beside me too.

One smoke allowed for the manic inhalation of craving but would have been over far too soon. Two smokes was a deep sigh of relief with time to relax, enjoy and calm down while three left us gagging, wanting to clean our teeth and swearing we'd never imbibe in that dubious pleasure again. Life could be so perfect!

We sat there puffing on our fags, slurping that yearned for one and only cold beer. Laughing with relief, laughing because after all the madness everything was OK, but most of all, laughing at ourselves. There was no doubt about it - we were utterly mad!

I was bruised, battered and sore and my feet were blistered and raw. My hair looked like a birds nest it had so many twigs and leaves in it from laying so long writhing and groaning in the dirt, yet even in that moment if I'd been given a choice to turn back the clock and have the life I used to live, I wouldn't have. No way! Oh yeah, I was being pushed to extremes every day. Nothing was turning out as I'd imagined it would, but Gill and I were laughing more than ever. After too many mundane years, we'd never felt so alive and I was loving it.

Of course I was mortified when Gill told me later what had happened to Zu. Gill had caught him in time and Zu was fine, but I felt so shameful that I'd made such a stupid mistake. I would have never been able to forgive myself if a camel, or any animal had died because of me.

It wasn't until much later in the night after Gill had gone to bed that the emotional impact of Kunkaa's kick really hit me.

I'd plonked myself down in the dirt with my back against the trunk of the huge desert oak that sheltered our camp. I had suddenly felt so frail, I wanted to feel the strength of this ancient tree whose roots went deep into the heart of the earth and whose trailing fronds whispered in the softest of breeze. Perhaps if I listened hard enough or relaxed enough, I was never quite sure which, I might just understand what she was saying when she whispered. Whatever language she spoke, I felt comforted sitting there.

Even though I'd spent the night sitting around the fire with Gill, laughing and happy, shock is something that ricochets and as I sat under that tree, I'd been surprised to find my body was still trembling. All these tears surfaced and I began to sob. I felt so vulnerable and so fragile. If I had been more seriously injured, Kunkaa's kick could have ended our entire trip, even my life, *and* the life of our camel king, Zu.

As I gazed into the last embers of our dying fire, while moonlight danced like filigree under the gently waving fronds of the oak, I knew I'd been given a powerful lesson and one I could *never* ignore again. I did not have the luxury of inattention. I *had* to be totally present when handling our camels in *every* situation. No excuses. We *would* face exhaustion again, this trip would challenge us every single day but we had all these animals depending on us and we had to travel at a pace that didn't push Gill or I over the edge - that was the big mistake we'd made. I'd felt exhausted hours before we pulled up. We should have stopped then. If our camels didn't get a great feed one night, we would stop in good feed the next. If we went through sparse days where there was little feed around, we would pull up and camp for days when we reached lush feed again. It would be a constant juggle to keep balance but the force that had propelled us on this trip was so strong, we had to trust we would find a way to keep all our animals healthy and fed and ourselves looked after too.

It felt like winter had well and truly fled when we woke early the next day to unfamiliar morning warmth. The camels were still disgruntled. They'd finally but begrudgingly nibbled the branches of the oaks after ascertaining that no other tempting morsels would be coming their way. As we harnessed up we were not a happy bunch of campers. A herd of hungry and difficult camels, my face all tender and bruised and Gill and I both still felt very tired. After the lesson from the night before, we decided to travel *only* until we reached some feed and prayed we would find some soon.

We passed Ewaninga Rock carvings that day - stunning outcrops of rocks that loomed on the east of the track, breaking up the horizon with their deep red buttressed craggy formations, all holey and gnarled like Swiss cheese. The track was climbing slightly and had lost its hard surface. The wheels of the wagon constantly sunk in the deep sand and the camels hefted inch by inch under a sun that was getting hotter, burning my winter skin with its unexpectedly fierce glare. We spent hours endlessly digging our wagon out of thick sand and no sooner had we freed it, it got bogged again up to its axle. I thought the day before had been bad, this was even worse. When Gill wasn't digging the wagon out of deep sand he'd be working the camels with his voice. Giving them all commands to 'pull em up, pull em up'. I was amazed at his capacity to vocalise with such ferocity for so long. I'd only managed five minutes before my voice became dry and croaky.

When we finally reached the crest of a slight rise, a whole day had passed and we decided to pull up and camp. We'd slogged the whole day and travelled less than a kilometre and could almost see the camp fire from the night before. The feed wasn't abundant but after last night's frugal offerings, it would appear to our camels as a feast.

And once again we were rolling along in our getting very familiar routine of unharnessing the camels, tethering them out, feeding all our other beasties and finally, with everyone happily munching and some serenity restored in camp, walking all our dogs. We had finally reached that ached for time of day when we both gave a big sigh of relief that the jobs were all done and we could finally focus on US and were about to collapse into our fancy camp chairs, when we saw our next big challenge. Our billy hadn't even boiled for our earl grey tea and my biggest fear was looming.

Standing on the other side of the fence we were camped alongside was a wild bull camel and he looked big, frothy and mean.

My heart did the biggest lurch. We had finally come face to face with that dreaded and yet much anticipated moment in time when we all we could do was grab the shot gun and while feeling absolutely knackered, try and do our best impersonation of a mad and really wild bull camel and pray it was terrifying enough to scare the shit out of him and have him running for his dear little life. That was the plan anyway, but some of our female camels were being much more inviting and flirting with this bull over the fence. Zu was bubbling froth like all good bulls do, pacing up and down frustrated he couldn't get over to this rival male and fight it out. We definitely wanted to avoid that showdown.

I felt pretty safe with the fence between us, but we had heard so many stories of thwarted bulls breaking through them that we didn't want to take a chance. I didn't want to take *any* chances. Wild bulls were my biggest fear and we had been totally indoctrinated with horror stories which had led me to view them as an outback version of King Kong. I knew we had to act fast, and mustering up unknown morsels of strength we raced over to him, flapping our arms and shouting in an attempt to get him to retreat away from our camels.

I felt so sorry for Gill as I watched him duck through the fence with shotgun in tow and disappear into the red blaze of the day's last light as he chased the little rotter. I paced the fence for a while myself, unwilling to relax totally into my end of day slump. I could hear the sound of Gill's gunshots getting further and further away. I hadn't realised he would chase him so far. Zu, with the opposition gone, had finally stopped pacing had begun to eat the food around him.

I chopped up vegetables and got dinner on to cook as I waited anxiously for Gills return. The red colours of the sunset had almost faded into the night when I saw the silhouette of him looming out of the darkness with his gun slung over his shoulder. I felt so proud of my man, my hero who'd saved us all from 'the attack of the wild bull' and as he got closer, I could see he was smiling and relaxed. I was about to run towards him when I noticed something moving in the bush behind him that he obviously hadn't seen.

"That's sorted him out," Gill told me confidently and with a slight swagger, a little puffed up with the discovery of his previously untapped ability to terrify wild bull camels. Yet unbeknown to Gill, creeping up behind him, sneaking from bush to bush all the way back was that wild bull he thought he'd scared away. The rotter had followed Gill all the way home.

The pleasure of a cup of earl grey tea at the end of a ravaging day cannot be indefinitely delayed. Gill had neither the energy or the inclination to chase that bull again and his only remaining destination for that night was his camp chair. We would have to trust in the fence. If he broke through it then we would look at the situation again. Zu was a little stirred up again but other than that, it all felt pretty calm and our girls were *loving* this new man and the flirtations continued over the fence.

We'd worked out we had only travelled thirty kilometres since we left on the trip and yet every rugged step had been an epic adventure. We felt as if we'd climbed mountains using our bare hands to wedge in the cracks and risked our lives to swim rivers with currents that could sweep away a whole town, and yet we had survived it all.

We just had to keep going and the words *it's got to get easier* was becoming our mantra.

Twenty

Holy Heck

We slept that night like worn out babes and I don't think anything would have enticed us from our sleep, so it was a relief to awaken and find the wild bull sitting peacefully, chewing his cud and still on the *other* side of the fence.

Our crew were all so much happier with their bellies full. Even the goats jumped into their wagon all by themselves and harnessing all the camels flowed with an unfamiliar ease. Lady Caroline still liked to do her queenly promenade alongside the wagon before being harnessed herself. We couldn't cut her walk short, speed it up, or even approach the wagon with her from a different direction. It had to be the same routine every day and if we obliged it took five minutes - if we didn't, all blooming day!

Even the chickens were clucking contentedly as they jostled for front row seats. If they sat close to the mesh at the front of their home they had a much better view out as we travelled along. Our beloved rooster The Colonel was such a gentleman, his girls always came first and he always took a back-row seat. I'd heard many cameleers say their chickens had barely laid eggs when they'd travelled with them in their wagons. Ours were laying prolifically, but we were *very* attentive to their needs. As we walked alongside the wagon we always gathered wild plants they loved to eat and threw them in. I always felt deeply satisfied when I peeped in and saw them happily sitting in a bed of flowers, their fragrant nibbles for along the way. And every day we made sure we pulled up and camped early enough in the day for them to have some time out. Happy chickens were as much a goal as happy camels.

The wild bull was still sitting quietly when we gave our camel team the command to 'pullem up, pullem up', accompanied by the eardrum shattering screeches of our parrots and the accompanying hoo-hah of howls and barks from our excited dogs. When he saw us take off, he followed for a while along the fence line but when the track veered away from the fence we lost him. I was sad to see him go, knowing he was all alone, but happy we'd dealt with our first wild bull encounter so peacefully.

It was a beautiful day. The track was still deep sand and corrugated too, but the camels were full of energy and raring to go and they moved through the sand with ease and speed, jogging for miles with me running along in the lead, easily maintaining the pace. We were in this wonderful flow and our bodies were all feeling fitter. Oh, what happiness when we saw thickets of spiky acacia victoria covered in yellow blossoms, one of the camel's favourite foods that always left their breath sweet and fragrant like its flowers. The red earth was also covered in tiny little papery yellow flowers that looked dried up and tasteless yet the camels would vacuum them up as if they were delicious treats.

This was the first morning we experienced a really connected flow with all our animals and it gave us both such a thrill. We were *actually* doing it. This thing we'd slaved for, hauling ourselves over and through every single obstacle, never giving up, believing in the impossible, unwilling to accept any limitation even our own, and it had led to this blissed out moment in time where we were all moving through the landscape as one - Gill and I laughing and happy, the camels feeling so good they just wanted to run and run and unfit me was running like the wind beside them.

Every day was a constant unfurling of confidence but even in this high I didn't want to get blasé. I couldn't take anything for granted. I know from past experiences that I was most likely to crash at the very moment I thought I'd gotten a handle on something, those little ego moments when you rise up like a star, all confident and full of yourself and then crash land flat on your face.

I was grateful when the pace slowed because the scenery was exquisite. All around us were huge sand dunes, deep terracotta red baked in sunshine with all sorts of bushes and flowers - silver cassias with their bright yellow buttercups and colony wattles heavy with golden blossoms. I was bush starved and I couldn't soak up enough of this country.

Even though we were working so hard, I could already feel such a release from being away from TV with its depressing drone of the news and its comatose reality shows that always seemed to suck me in. For too many years I'd lived in a haze of static energy, too much time on the computer, or sitting in front of a sewing machine. Living outside in nature with all our animals was invigorating. I felt so much clearer and I revelled in feeling my unfit body stretch out and grow stronger as each day passed. My capacity to keep going seemed to have no end. There were many moments I felt I'd reached my limit, only to have it vigorously tested each time and discover that I could always go beyond. There was always more of me to give and that knowing blew me away. Until this time, I'd always stopped at feeling tired. That was surely the time to rest and recharge and yet this experience was showing me how each time I pushed through tiredness, I expanded my energy and reached untapped resources I'd never known I had. As I was discovering, this was not a trip for anyone who rested at the first hurdle!

After yesterday's sorrowful progress I'd woken up with very low expectations of how far we'd travel and yet here we were striding out, the kilometres whipping past like sand blowing in a dust storm across the desert and it felt so good.

As I strode out along the track I could see a mountain of a dune towering over on my left, and on the other side was a parked ute and a guy was just unloading two small kiddies quad bikes. When he saw us coming, he settled himself on the bonnet of his vehicle to sit and watch us pass, slurping from his early morning beer. When we stopped to say hello, he was shaking his head in disbelief and muttering, "Unbelievable."

Gill jumped down from the wagon and I tucked the lead rope into Zu's harness so it didn't fall around his feet and we went over to say hello. The funny thing with our camels was they would stand and look like little angels whenever we stopped to chat with a tourist. It was hard for anyone to even imagine that many were wild and untrained, let alone dangerous. They made our whole procession look as if we had it completely under control and as if they were all perfectly trained.

As we stood chatting with this man and his two young sons I was singing our camels praises when all of a sudden, something happened that turned my blood cold.

On the other side of the wagon was the huge sand dune. It towered above the track it was so high, and sliding sideways down it and out of control was our old mate from the night before, the wild bull camel. He had never left us, he'd followed the fence line looking for a weak spot and had broken through. There was me, foolishly thinking we'd dealt with him with such ease.

He came hurtling down that hill with such speed and then threw himself into the middle of our two lines of harnessed camels. I could not have imagined a worse scenario. If our camels panicked, we could end up with a huge tangled mess of camels and chains. My heart literally stopped for a moment in panic and yet I found myself calmly going through the motions, grabbing the reins and talking softly to our camels to keep them calm. All the time I was aware of Gill jumping into the wagon, getting the shot gun and the cattle prod before leaping out. His every move was urgent and, in his rush, he forgot to put the wagons brake on. As the bull camel in the midst of our harnessed team began to thrash around trying to manoeuvre our camels away, the wagon lurched forward. Gill had no choice but to quickly climb back in and secure the brake before he tackled this bull.

I remained calm as I kept reassuring the camels, but inside I felt sick with fear. This was the stuff of my worst nightmares and it was happening. While I had illusions I was helping to calm the camels, it was much more likely they were holding a grounding and anchored space for me. They didn't appear phased *at all* by what was happening. In fact, our beloved adorable angels of camels stood perfectly still and didn't move at all as Gill climbed in around them, slipping inbetween the chains, getting as close to the bull as he could to try and zap him on the mouth with the cattle prod. It was the last thing we wanted to do - we love all animals, but we couldn't risk him hurting our animals. We were dealing with a bull driven by testosterone. His only focus was our girls.

Using the cattle prod was a huge and freaky risk but we couldn't see any other way. If it backfired we'd be in big trouble. Of course we didn't want to stir him up and make him stroppy, but we had to get him out from all the chains that our camels harnesses were clipped on to before he caused them harm. I held my breath feeling sick as I watched this drama unfold and I felt so sorry for that bull. When Gill prodded him, he leapt in the air so high and miraculously, hallelujah, praise the lord, landed on the other side of the wagon, freed from the midst of our camel team. It was an unbelievable transformation of a dire situation. He could have barged, but he leapt! I was so relieved, but that prod had not put him off and he began circling us predaciously, running around us all, bellowing loudly as he tried to find another way to separate some of our girls. I tell you it was frightening.

Throughout all of this the guy with the kids had been sitting on his car bonnet, still slurping his beer, watching our camel drama unfold with a slightly flabbergasted look on his face while his two young kids stood nearby watching. All were completely unaware that this bull could get dangerous and it would be wise for them to position themselves in a safe place. Gill yelled at him urgently to put the kids up on the car. The bull had already done a few laps around them and was getting more pissed off.

I was so glad we'd been paranoid enough to buy a whole arsenal of tools. Gill began cracking his stock whip in an attempt to drive the bull further away so he could then use the shot gun. Never with any intention to harm him, only to fire in the air or on the ground and scare him away.

And once again in a moment that we needed help it arrived - a couple of friends who'd come down to visit and deliver some drums of water had been parked a little further down the track when they heard the gun shots. They arrived like the calvary and took off after this bull, chasing him down the track for several kilometres in their 4WD until they were sure he wouldn't come back.

There was nothing dull about our new life. When our serenity was restored Gill and I had stood holding on to one another, legs still trembling, giddy with adrenalin and feeling so high. Our onlooker and his kids cheered as if they were at the footy when the bull began to retreat. He'd never seen such a fascinating spectacle and was so thankful he'd pulled into that layby at that exact moment in time and seen a sight he would most likely never ever witness again. He couldn't wait to tell his friends, but he wasn't sure anyone would believe him. We all laughed so much at that.

When we set off again I felt like we could cope with anything. It had been a huge adrenalin rush dealing with our first wild bull and I was so proud of our camels. They had been amazing. They had stood stoically looking ahead not paying the slightest attention to the bull that had thrown himself into their midst, even behaving as if he wasn't there. What blew me out the most though was Zu. I had seen him the night before. I'd watched him pacing restlessly because he knew a competitor was trying to lure his girls, and yet he seemed to have overridden all his testosterone driven instinct to get in and fight this bull. Instead he had stood calmly at the helm, holding such an anchored presence that the whole team had felt it. How blessed and fortunate were we to have such a noble animal keeping us all on track. Our camels never ceased to amaze me and I was left feeling awed by them all. In that moment all their sins were forgiven - all the struggling we had done trying to get them tied off the wagon, all the times they had bucked and kicked and dragged us around, they'd even had us flying through the air on the end of their ropes a few times but *none* of that mattered.

They were our precious little darlings and I loved them all.

We pulled up that night under more desert oaks, spread out eagled, majestic and proud. It was a picturesque place to camp and our friends were already there setting up a bucket in a tree we could shower under, lighting the fire and getting dinner ready. We were about to be fed and get clean.

You would have thought that after the challenges of the last few days I had learnt my lessons well. Apparently not.

Gill and I were unharnessing the camels and my cocky little self was being blasé and boastful about the challenges we had already faced since living this gruel of a dream. I was strutting around as if I had everything under control and there was nothing I couldn't deal with, when Zu unexpectedly lurched towards Kushy, our young and cheeky bullock and knocked me to the ground. I fell under his feet and rolled so fast to get out the way, only just missing being trodden on by a camel that weighed almost a tonne. It wasn't Zu's fault, it was mine and I was well and truly shunted back to earth from the high I'd been surfing that day. A kick in the face and a hugely swollen cheek was obviously not enough to teach me to stay present and focused on the job at hand. I should have known better. Zu had controlled all his natural instincts to be there when we needed him most and was bound to be feeling extra protective of his girls, and there was no excuse for my lack of awareness. I felt like an idiot and plunged from heroine to humiliated in one swift move.

After all the jobs were done I went for a walk, heading out to climb a dune and watch the sun set. I needed time to sit and chill on my own and get earthed. My energy was all over the place and had swung like a pendulum between despair and extreme joy since the day we'd left.

Everything looked so serene from high up on the dune as I sat watching the animals grazing and life unfolding in the valley below. The chickens were running about camp scratching up the earth in their search for grubs. The goats were all grazing around our camp. Our friends were dragging wood over to our camp fire and I watched them build up the kindling and kneel before it, coaxing it into life. It smouldered for a while before bursting into flames and soft tendrils of smoke were wisping and weaving around our camp and up into the sky.

I could see Gill in the distance exploring the bush with his faithful Bella, walking so close she looked like she was attached. She often drove Gill mad, she was never happy unless she had his sleeve in her mouth or the tails of his shirt to hang on to. She followed him everywhere and gave him no space and I could imagine Gill's grumblings as they walked,

"Get off Bella, leave me alone, stop that, and come on get out of my way." It was a strange love they shared, but it was love.

I felt so far away from everything as I sat on that dune and it was so good to get some distance. There was rarely any peace in camp and even if all the animals were feeding and happy, my body was always alert. How could I relax when I had no idea what was going to happen from one moment to the next? I never knew when some animal drama would have me jumping up from a moment's relaxation - I'd been surfing the highs and tumbling with the lows and I needed to find the balance inbetween. The highs were so high they had me spinning all over the place and the lows were plummets into gloom and despair. *Breathe Kye, remember to breathe. It will all get easier.*

High up above me I heard two eagles calling and I watched them spiralling downward in the thermals before landing in the high branches of a giant gum tree. Everything was so red as the day came to its end - the still warm sand, the craggy peaks that loomed on the horizon and the huge sky that belittled and put everything into perspective glowed, as the sun sunk down on the day and the flames of the camp fire way off in the distance danced as red as the setting sun. I walked back down to our camp, stepping over flowers that grew from vines like tentacles, sprouting from the desert sand, catching up with Gill and Bella as they also made their way home.

There was nothing I could take for granted on this trip. There would be no more sinking comfortably into complacency, no cocky bursts of splendour as I preened my know it all feathers. This was about being present and staying focused and twice in two days I had only just avoided being seriously hurt.

Time to wake up Kye.

Twenty-one

Our Lucky Mascot, Three Toes

It's so easy to feel confident when you're in the midst of friends and back on our own again, I felt so vulnerable. When I told Gill how I felt, he gave me a big hug and reminded me it wouldn't take long for us to get back into our flow. We'd feel better then, and I knew he was right. In our few days of camping we'd had so much fun but had become less honed. All it had taken was a few beers the night before and we were both cloudy and sluggish to get going. We'd never been big drinkers anyway, just the occasional social occasion, and only drank on this trip when friends called by or a passing stranger gave us one for later. There was so much that needed our completely focused attention, we were in complete agreement that the beer had to go. It was knocking us around too much.

As I walked out in front leading the camels I felt so insignificant in the harsh and ancient landscape that had witnessed many like us come and go with the years. The itinerant workers that had pushed wheelbarrows thousands of kilometres with all their worldly goods to the next place of work, settlers with their wagons loaded with household goods and kids sitting high on top, with the sheep and cattle being mustered along beside them as they set out into a country that was new to find land to farm that they could call their own.

We also trod the same well-worn tracks as the old Afghani cameleers who, until the car took over, had bought much needed provisions to the outback, their camel teams loaded to the hilt.

But there were no fellow travellers now. All that was left was the faintest echo of the past - a rusty hobble strap, a worn thin pearl button or a broken clay pipe. I would have loved to have seen this route as it was then, sat down under a tree with someone we'd just met and shared a meal and a story or two, or helped someone mend the broken spokes of a wagon wheel that had held a family up for days as they sheltered from the sun under the only tree for miles.

We walked silently, lost in our own thoughts with just the sounds of the camels bells clanking and jangling their melody of different notes. Soon the track we followed became one with the old disused railway line and the sides unexpectedly fell steeply away, leaving us a knife-like ridge to navigate and get all our animals safely across. There was no other route we could take and we didn't even have enough room to turn around and go back. We *had* to do this.

We were being tested everyday with something new, something to weaken the bowels and get those stomach muscles churning and this ridge that stretched for as far as we could see did a really good job of that. Our entourage was wide. We had camels tied from the side and those walking tethered from the back often walked wide of the wagon so they could see the road ahead. I didn't want to focus on the fact we could fall from the edge, but I couldn't help recognising that as a possibility. It was so daunting. I not only worried we would all fall, it was not until we had started our journey across that we realised there were sections of the track that had been washed away, leaving only just enough room to pass. It was sheer nail-biting horror and required total focus in each moment, and I all I could do was keep reminding myself to breathe and *trust*. I just kept holding that vision of us all happily on the other side, even though I felt fear.

Our camels were amazing. This motley and adorable crew of misfits that had come to be our tribe walked across that freaky ridge calmly and undaunted and without being naughty once. Even the wilder ones that were tethered from the back of the wagon walked across calmly, restraining from biting each other on the bum or hustling for a better position. I was still trembling with fear when we reached the other side but I felt sick with relief that we'd made it.

That night we camped in a field of yellow flowers under the only tree for miles - a squat gidgee tree with its rustling silvery leaves. We soon realised the yellow flowers were not edible for our camels, but it all looked so pretty we prayed they would find something else to tempt them amidst this decadent beauty. On the horizon was the Ooramina Range, the hugest red knarled rock formations that nestled like some ancient dinosaur sleeping.

I got out my camera. I couldn't resist and lay on my belly in the flowers taking pictures of everything, the goats coming up and peering in my lens while Blossom and the other young camels Jali and Windy cavorted playfully together. Everything looked so beautiful, the smoke of the camp fire climbing skyward and mingling with the rays of the setting sun that cast its last light on a field of yellow tops with their feathery crowns and the billy buttons that grew in their midst, all swaying in the faint breeze like a rippling lake.

We set off early the next day, following the huge camel prints of another solitary bull that had also used this track and going by the freshness of the prints, not so long ago. The dirt road led through scraggly mulga trees and was as near to travelling through a forest as the desert can give, and at each bend in the track we looked expectantly for signs of the beast that we followed. We were like wild animals ourselves listening, watching all hackled and alert, noticing the bushes he had fed from with their broken down branches and the leaves stripped clean, the trampled ground where he had passed an hour or two resting in the shade with its fresh still steaming dung.

But all we saw that day was four American tourists that jumped out of the bush like misplaced people with huge cameras and video recorders, asking us to speak into the video like we were making a documentary or sending a personal message to our families at home. It was a rude awakening to the reverie we had fallen into, the silent stillness we had found as we walked quietly through the bush, not separate but part of it all. I felt grubby and disheveled as I tried to be polite and find the part of me that knew how to communicate and could deal with this rowdy exchange that demanded and didn't give and failed to sense our wild fragility, like startled beasts caught in a spotlight.

I enjoy people, but just then I think we had both flown so far away that it was hard to come back down to earth and answer a monologue of questions. Questions we would answer, always the same, rarely changing for the rest of the trip. Our camels stood like little well-behaved angels once again and behaved with such grace and charm, it looked like we were miracle workers when the American Tourists exclaimed at what a wonderful job we had done when we told them thirteen of our camels were practically wild. After saying a farewell message into the video for the 'folks back home in the States', we once again got on our way, still watching the meandering tracks of the camel we followed, fresh and sharp in the sand.

Blossom and Bella had been wandering freely behind the wagon with Lulu, Windy, Jumuna and Jali, the feeding mums that needed to eat as much as they could as we travelled along, but we decided to tie them all onto the wagon and have everyone safe and close. We were still following the solitary tracks of a wild bull and wanted to be ready for the unexpected. These wild bulls certainly added a daunting edge to the so far already perilous adventure we were on. But as the day passed his trail veered off to the east and we began to relax a little and look out for a camp. We'd already travelled further than intended in the promissory pursuit of good feed and when we came across a place that didn't have great feed but had enough to keep our grumbling camels happy, we decided to pull up for the night.

Every day we were refining the art of unharnessing the camels and getting all our animals fed and watered and cared for before we sat down. We always did the camels first and got the biggest animals out of the way. Then we opened the door of the little wagon so all the goats could jump out. When all the bigger animals were out of the way we set the ladder in place and let the chickens out. They would alight from their carriage with such eagerness to explore. Every day they had fresh terrain and new dust holes to role in and they were thriving in their life on the road. Next, we'd let the doves out for a fly, feed and water the parrots and then it was the dogs turn.

The dogs had to be constantly on a lead because of baits. We'd tried to muzzle them, but they writhed and struggled the entire time they wore them. I always felt a little afraid the muzzles would come off and I couldn't trust them with my dogs lives. In the end, we discarded the muzzles and each morning covered our bed in canvas so it didn't get dirty and the dogs sat on that. They could hang out the windows of our wagon, bark at passing cars and grab leaves from the trees when we skimmed too close. It was all a huge adventure for them and they loved it. Periodically throughout the day they each came out for a walk on a lead, but it was on one of our pre-dusk dog walks that Gill and I began playing a silly game. It made us laugh so much and shifted the monotony of this routine. In our best sports commentators voices the game was on, and whoever's dog performed the best was the winner.

And they are over the starting line, it's Patchi and Wunjo and they're doing their first sniff of the terrain. These two have been good performers in the past, so either could take the lead and pee first. OH MY GOODNESS It looks like Wunjo is sniffing the bush! Is that a squat? Oh no, she's changing her mind. It looks like a false start, she's not quite ready. A huge disappointment for Kye there who thought she was about to take the lead. Wunjo is looking like she needs to sniff a little more, but the delay has cost her and it looks as if Patchi has taken the lead. He's cocked his leg and yes! It's a cracker of a pee. Oh my goodness everyone that's a fabulous pee from Patchi. Another solid performance from this dog who never lets us down and it's Patchi in the lead, but can Wunjo recover from this?

We'd just got all the jobs done for the night and reached that wonderful moment when dinner was cooking on the fire and the billy was boiled for a cup of tea when we saw him.

The most ginormous king of a beast, splendid in all his frothy maleness standing, thankfully once again for what it's worth, on the other side of the fence and watching us all with a noble dignity that I didn't even want to chase away, let alone shoot. *Please, please beautiful camel, just behave yourself, please.*

He was so magnificent, we both felt compelled to gently walk to the fence line to have a closer look. Zu was calmly eating and appeared unbothered by our guest who wasn't at all perturbed by our approach. "Hey look," said Gill, "He's got three toes," and sure enough he had an extra toe, instead of the two toes that camels normally have. We laughed about it being a sign of good luck like a four leafed clover, and decided to let him be and go and sit down and enjoy our much-earned cup of tea.

Three toes, our lucky mascot, didn't bother us at all that night and was still there in the morning, sitting a little distance away enjoying the warmth of the sun. He was so beautiful and I hoped he'd find a herd and I wished he could have come with us, but neither of us reckoned we could cope with anymore challenges. One bull camel was enough.

The only miracle of this new day was that the goats jumped into their wagon unaided, it was a small respite for the barrage of a day that was about to unfold and wrap its dregs around us. This day we had the camel team from hell. All five of them were bent on subverting the course of our flow, leaving the track and heading bush at the slightest opportunity, getting the wagon stuck in soft deep sand and then ignoring our requests, then our firm voiced commands and finally our yelling, red faced, blood vessels bursting hysterical orders to get those goddamn lazy buts moving and back on the track. They stared at us like we had gone mad, casually chewing their cud like a piece of gum with not a care in the world, completely untouched by our hysteria.

Each time we got stuck in the sand it took us hours and hours to dig the wagon out. It was utterly exhausting and when the wagon lurched forward finally free, it was a momentous moment of jubilation. The sheer relief, the cheering, the jumping up and down whooping with joy and high fiving each other that we were finally on our way again. Then no sooner had we reached the hard surface of the track and taken a few paces, they left the track again and got us bogged in even deeper sand. FUCK FUCK FUCK. FUUUUUUUUCK! I was so fucking mad. We faced hours of digging again in the hot sun, my lips were dried out and salt blasted, my clothes were dripping and stank of sweat. I fucking couldn't take a moment more of this hellish trip and I was certain the camels were leaving the road on purpose.

Zu, in the lead and guiding the whole rebellion, had his mouth hanging open in a goofy look of surprise, as if he couldn't quite figure out how we'd ended up bogged again. Our camels had shown us over and over again how intelligent they were and while Zu was pretending to be stupid, I had absolutely no doubt he was not.

I was so glad that we'd not accepted an offer from the several made for someone to come and film us. I could see the headlines now: *The truth about Kye and Gill, the so called animal lovers, who died of exhaustion only seventy kilometers down the track.* I'd turned my life inside out to care for our camels and all these animals, even taking on dangerous and skeletal camels that no-one else in their right mind would, and look where our kindness had gotten us.

We travelled several tortured kilometres that hacked every morsel of energy from our already feeble supplies and when we finally pulled into camp, I was in the wildest rage. I was so mad, I didn't know what to do with myself for my own safety. If there'd been a lovers leap anywhere close I would have thrown myself into oblivion from its edge. Instead I paced around, wanting to smash everything and hurl all our camping gear into the bush and let out the most blood curdling scream. It was only the fear of attracting tourists that held that banshee call in.

I was furious with Gill, I felt like throttling him. I *could not* believe that I'd let him persuade me into selling my lovely home and leave on this maniacal adventure and in that moment, I loathed my beloved as much as I loathed the camels.

Exhausted, I slumped down onto the ground, into the dirt and dust and the next moment, I was screaming. The ground was covered in vicious prickles that pierced my flesh like I'd been stabbed with a bayonet. FUCK. Everything was just getting worse. Whatever I focused on in my world looked bleak and despairing. All I wanted was to go home, run a hot bath and settle down on the couch and watch a movie, but home was long gone and that thought had me sobbing in grief and prickle punctured pain.

I climbed into the wagon feeling so sorry for myself and lay on the bed screaming into my pillow, kicking at the ceiling and all the while trying to formulate an escape plan. I *had* to get away. *Could I catch a taxi back to town? Would they drive seventy odd kilometers down a corrugated dirt road to get me? Could I leave Gill with all these animals on his own? Well he's the arsehole that got me into this, YES I damn well could, the bastard!*

I fumed and screamed until I wore myself out and I lay on the bed *absolutely* spent. I was filthy dirty again and had more twigs and leaves in my tangled outback mess of hair. I was sunburnt, my eyes were all puffy and my face was streaked with dirt and snot where I'd cried and cried. I was well and truly rocking self-pity when my beloved bought me a cup of earl grey tea, and the fucker was smiling!

My absolutely infuriating wild bushman can also be so romantic. After I'd drunk my tea, he told me to come with him - he wanted to show me something. He led me by the hand out of our camp, past our camels who I am sure were giving me wry little grins, to a huge red sand dune and together we climbed to the top to watch the sunset. Sitting in amongst clumps of desert hearth myrtle and trails of ants we could see for miles across that mesmerisingly magnificent red duned land and everything began to feel so tranquil and calm. Surprisingly, even me.

We were both happy to see some huge water tanks nearby. Our next mission was to find water and fill all the tanks on our wagon, and it was a relief that we didn't have far to travel. We sat on that dune in the amber glow of the day's last light watching the animals feeding below. The fairytale illusion of our lives looked idyllic from our great height. When Gill put his arm around me and pulled me close I really wasn't prepared for what he had to say.

"It's a bloody good holiday isn't it, let's come back again next year."

My mouth fell open in shock and I just looked at him in astonishment. After the hell I'd just gone through, I couldn't believe what he'd said. He had such a cheeky grin on his face and we just stared at each other for a moment before we both cracked up laughing and once we started, we couldn't stop. We were laughing so much we were rolling around in the sand holding our aching bellies, tears were rolling down my face and in that moment, I couldn't have cared less if I'd peed myself.

Twenty-two

The Travelling Lovefest

The next day we had the camel team from heaven. They rose like little angels, all eager to please, reaching down to smooch us as they inveigled their way back into our good books and Gill and I, like little gullible puppies, walked along beside them singing their praises as they beamed lovingly at us. Yesterday was already long gone.

We planned to travel to the water tank, pull the wagon up to the tanks as close as we could, siphon the water into our big tanks underneath the wagon and while our tanks were filling, bucket some water for the camels so they could all have a drink at the same time.

To get to the tanks we had to leave the track we were on and travel a few kilometres along the main dirt road. Finally, all in position, Gill dropped the hoses into the water and as the water began to flow into our tanks we found ourselves distracted by a really loud noise. An exhaustless car was coming down the road in our direction. I prayed it would keep on going. It was making so much noise that all the animals were getting uneasy. The only sounds we'd had in our lives since we'd left had been natural. The wind, the sounds of the birds, me screaming, stuff like that! I had to always remind myself to laugh.

We'd been giving our camels regular small daily drinks but as the days had begun to get hotter, they were wanting more water. Now I know people will tell you that camels can go for long periods without water and it's true, but they don't do it willingly. You have to train them into it. We'd heard of some people trekking with camels who'd got them used to only drinking water every few days, some even longer. They are desert creatures and built to survive in a parched land, but naturally if water is there they will drink it and if the weather is hot, they will seek it out. Our trip wasn't about survival. We wanted happy camels. We had no desire to push them to the edges of their physical endurance. If our bubs wanted water, water they had and they were all eager for a drink. This created a massive challenge for us that we hadn't anticipated.

They were all reaching for our buckets at the same time and we only had two. Siphoning the water wasn't happening fast enough and they were all getting jumpy and excited at the prospect of a drink. As soon as we'd filled our buckets, several camels were competing for a drink and either knocking it over or getting tangled. It was also very dangerous for us if we didn't totally focus and I felt really alarmed when the exhaustless car that we'd heard making the most awful din pulled up right beside us and all our camels.

We were doing our best to settle our camels down when all the car doors flew open and aboriginals from the nearby community, just returning from partying in town fell out in great numbers, all in various states of non-compos mentis. They were staggering along the ground, eyes all bleary and red, some holding themselves up on others, but they all had one thing in common. They were a travelling lovefest.

One of our inebriated visitors staggered up to Andaria, who, while she is one of the most intelligent and wisest creatures I have ever met is not that effusive - and why should she be? Animals are just like us and many don't like being touched by strangers. Andaria looked horrified as this guy wrapped his arms around her neck, almost hanging from her while kissing her passionately and saying, "I love you, I love you, I love you." It was hard work trying to extrapolate him from his new-found love and no sooner had I succeeded, he was staggering over to

Mozzee, who at least would be up for a good old hug.

These party goers were swarming all over our camels like ants. Gill and I were running around like panicked parents trying to stop them going too close to the wild camels on the back, grabbing the foot of another as he tried to shuffle on his hands and knees under their legs. *Oh my God, please let no one get hurt.* I felt so stressed. Dealing with all these drunken people was more challenging then my biggest fear, wild bull camels.

One man was even passionately snogging Bella like she was a long lost love - a big no no! She had her ears back, looking ferocious and Gill was yelling urgently, "That's a cheeky donkey that one, watch out, cheeky one, cheeky one!" Cheeky one was the term used by the aboriginals for an animal that could bite or kick but even with this warning, in their drunken haze, the severity of our words went unheeded. They were going up and cuddling animals that would have booted a more sober man and I'm sure it was only their unguarded innocence and love for the animals that kept them safe.

Their entire visit was fraught with peril as we ran around trying to keep an eye on what they were doing and it was such a relief when they finally packed themselves like sardines back into their car, with stray legs and arms hanging out the windows and started up, breaking all reasonable noise levels as they drove off, yelling affectionately above the din.

"See ya sister, see ya brother," they called and we probably would see them further down the track as we were heading their way. I felt so relieved when they'd gone!

It took us several hours to fill up and water our animals. A long, slow and arduous process that didn't have me looking forward to the next time we had to do it, but finally we returned along the road to rejoin the old Ghan line. We always looked for the old rusty nails called dog spikes that littered the ground where the old railway had been pulled up. These were our constant markers that always told us we were on the right track.

The track was washed out with several big rocky dry creek beds to navigate across. We were still exhausted after yesterday's shenanigans and decided to pull up under a short, fat, burly ghost gum and spend a few days catching up with washing and baking food that we could eat as we travelled.

We'd got into a routine of stopping every third day unless we were travelling through country with really poor feed, then we continued until we reached a better place to stop. There were always so many jobs that needed to be done and a few days being stationary gave us a chance to catch up on washing our filthy clothes. We did it all by hand in big buckets with the essential tool - a scrubbing brush. Then we'd hang them to dry in the branches of the trees and they'd look like prayer flags waving in the breeze. The sun bleached the stains that we thought would never come clean and at the end of the day it was such a good feeling to have fresh clothes to wear again.

While our washing was drying we'd stoke up the camp fire and bake chick pea patties, nut loaves and cakes in a camp oven in the coals, food we could eat during the day when we travelled. Every morning began with bowl of porridge topped with dried fruit and nuts and we always cooked an evening meal. We had a range of meals we could make, from pumpkin soup and homemade bread, to vegetable bakes or a lentil curry with poppadums. If we were absolutely knackered we opted for two-minute angel hair pasta with pesto and sun dried tomatoes, but we always had to prebake the food we'd eat during our day on the road. It was always food we could grab a big slice of and eat while on the run. One of my favorites was Gill's fruit and nut damper that was loaded with dates and walnuts, sultanas and almonds and was a slightly more bready version of Christmas cake.

We had just finished cooking our damper on the hot coals and thankfully taken all our clean clothes down from the branches when it began to gently rain. We were sure the clouds would soon pass over, but by the following morning when we'd hoped to travel on, the rain had really settled in and was pelting down. We moved our fire pit just inside our awning and out of the reach of the rain and sat huddled over its flames, eating and reading books for the next five days, until the leaves on the trees no longer dripped with the rain and the ground had dried up enough for us to travel on without getting bogged.

Our life on the road was so arduous that when we got a chance to be still we lapped it up. When you're moving it's easy to keep moving, but when you stop it takes huge effort to start again. We were all slow and lethargic the day we decided to leave. Every little job was a huge effort and when we finally set off, it was at a slow old plod.

We were learning every day to go with the pace that flowed. It was often challenging to let go of expectations and go with what was and not how we'd hoped it would be. We were all feeling slow, so slow was the pace of the day. It was easier than fighting and we'd all find our pace again.

Our track led out of the sand duned desert oak country and dipped down through several creek crossings edged with gum trees, that stood like silvery giants along our way. The camels began to trot as we travelled down these inclines and across dried out creeks, finding momentum to trot up the rises with ease. We hadn't gone very far that day when we came to an even steeper rise - the biggest little hill we'd ever tackled with our big entourage and I was a little daunted, but with encouragement the camels easily pulled the wagon to the top, where Zu refused to go any further. We tried everything to get Zu to 'walk it up' but nothing would persuade him to budge. He was adamant he was not leading the team down that hill. Zu was our king who led us all everywhere but nothing we did or said convinced him to change his mind. Eventually, with no other solution, we took him out of harness and tethered him to a tree until we'd safely made the descent. Perhaps Zu had the gift of foresight and perhaps he knew, unlike me, that the pace would be much too fast for him.

Gill was in the wagon riding the brake as we began our brisk descent. I was trotting out in front, holding Lady Caroline's and gentle Nev's lead ropes and trying to trot fast enough to stay ahead, but the pace just kept getting faster and faster.

"Pull on the fucking brake!" I was yelling with such an urgency and he didn't appear to hear me. I couldn't understand why he wasn't responding to my situation. He must have been able to see I was running really fast and struggling to stay ahead. I kept praying the wagon would slow down but I lost all hope of that when I heard Gill yelling, "Run Kye, run!" One little trip and I'd end up under the feet of the camels behind me and with a three tonne wagon hurtling down over the top. I'd been kicked in the face, endured intolerable conditions and absolute exhaustion and now I was running as fast as I could, faster than I'd ever run before, red faced and breathless for my life, with our camels running as fast as they could too. I knew I couldn't keep up my olympian pace for long and it was a split second decision to hurl myself into the bushes on the side of the track. If I wanted to see another day, this leap of faith was my only option and of course I landed in a spiky bush where, bleeding and scratched, I watched Gill thunder by not knowing if and when he would ever stop. He looked like a roman in an out of control chariot.

My best move had been leaping out of the way. Without me in the lead our camels had the good sense to veer off the side of the track into the soft sand where the whole caboodle came to a halt, stuck in bushes, with a fallen tree blocking the way. I was mad, more so because I'd been so afraid that

I or our camels or Gill would get hurt and I couldn't stop trembling. I was scratched and bloody with my hair full of twigs and leaves again. This was becoming *my* look.

I cuddled in Gill's arms until my shaking subsided. He'd been just as freaked out as me and not only because I could have been seriously injured, but for our animals too. He felt responsible for how the wagon performed. We'd both gone to every length to make sure every aspect of our animals well-being was cared for, even lining every head collar, every hobble strap, every harness with sheepskin so none of them would experience a sore from a rub. We'd thought we had covered everything, anticipated every potential crisis and it had not ever occurred to us that our wagon's brake would fail, putting us all in danger. And while I certainly didn't hold him responsible, the brake Gill had built was obviously not strong enough to slow the weight of our fully loaded wagon.

We both felt teary and vulnerable as we praised our team of camels, especially Lady Caroline and Nev for their heroic feat of guiding the wagon to a safe halt. They had made a split-second negotiation to change direction when the momentum of the wagon was hurtling down that track.

Their fast thinking had saved us all.

Twenty-three

Beautiful Faery Nev

There was no doubt our camels knew exactly how to push my every trigger, and yet every single time we needed them to step up, they did. I'd even had this sneaky suspicion that they pushed my triggers intentionally. While I always felt on the periphery of their secret camel business there was a sense of it I understood. There were glances that passed between them, wry little grins they couldn't keep hidden that I'd notice in my more explosive moments, when everything felt as if it was going wrong. *Just push her a little more, she needs to dump that shit* - and push me they would. A purposeful step in the wrong direction that bogged our wagon in deep sand, five seconds after we finally freed it after hours of digging it out in the hot sun. One little step, that's all it took to send me over the edge and have me bawling like a baby, face down in the dirt, a bloodied and blistered mess of self-pity, scratches and tangles. Yet even then I felt them, heard silent voices whispering in my head. *That's enough everyone, I don't think she can take much more today. Giver her a break now, we'll unload some more of her baggage another day but good going everyone, she certainly dumped a lot of her shit today.*

I always say it was no mistake that the wise men chose camels! Camels always know exactly what they are doing. These creatures surpass every limitation man has foolishly put on an animal and yet people can spend years with them and not truly see them. They won't even begin to let you in until *you're* ready and some people never are. Try and dominate them or abuse them and every door to these phenomenal beings remains shut. You have got to earn *their* respect, you have to step up and show them who you are and that you can meet them in honour, respect and integrity. That's why camels have often had a bad reputation, few of their handlers make the grade. Show these animals violence, dominate their every move, disrespect yourself so much that you cannot possibly respect them and you are shut out, possibly forever, from the sacred and beautiful realm of the camels.

In every moment they continued to surprise me. I was their student, it was never the other way around. How egotistic I had been to even think I had to train them, when it was me all along. As I stood by Nev and thanked him for bringing us all to safety, he bowed his big beautiful red face towards me. There was always an intensity in this camel's eyes, he let you see his depths. There was never anything hidden. This wise master, nursemaid to the young and the elderly, always felt like he'd come from a different realm than even our other camels. If the faerys had camels, Nev, with his other worldly beauty and his gentle and sensitive ways was one of them and as I met his gaze I was astounded by the communion that passed between us.

Beside me Gill was fussing over Lady Caroline. She relished being in the limelight. To be honoured by her beloved Gill for her part in bringing the wagon to safety was one of the highest accolades she could ever have hoped for. She looked so proud, but it was deep and sensitive Nev that shared something with me when I looked into his eyes that was unexpected.

We are as much a part of this trip as you and Gill are. What we do, we do together. The load is shared between us, the weight is not all on you.

On some level I had always felt this. After all, many of the camels had communicated to us *before* we'd even known they existed and the way most of the animals had come had been very serendipitous. They always made it clear they were meant to be there. Was it possible they had all chosen to come on this crazy adventure? That's what I'd always felt, yet the whole idea seemed preposterous even to me and yet here was Nev, letting me know that what we were all doing was indeed, shared. They had their part to play as much as we had ours but as I began to absorb Nev's communion, another question came to my mind. *Why are so many of the camels still resisting us?*

And the answer came to me immediately. *They are taking you and Gill to a place of surrender. Their resistance is your resistance. You wait and see, everything will shift when you both let go and that time will surely come.* I certainly felt a weight lift from me knowing that.

We reclaimed Zu from his perch on the hill where he'd watched the unfolding drama, no doubt patting himself on the back for his wise choice, though even that conclusion I thought at the time was likely to belittle him. I was in no doubt anymore that animals communicated telepathically and I'd come to realise that was how Andaria had known Kushy was in trouble when he'd had his foot tangled in barbed wire. Since that time, we'd had many examples of their telepathic communication with us and between themselves.

From Zu's vantage point at the top of the hill had he indeed guided Nev and Caroline in the safest course of action? It wouldn't have surprised me! Nor would it have surprised me to know that Zu had foreseen what was about to happen with our runaway wagon and had purposefully chosen the best vantage point to assist.

We unharnessed the rest of the camels from the wagon, tethered them to the trees nearby and started to dig. I'd screamed so many times in frustration at the amount of time we spent digging our wagon out of deep sand and yet I felt grateful. Deeply, deeply, blessedly grateful. Digging for hours was a small price to pay for safely negotiating an incident that could have been calamitous. My every shovel load of sand was a prayer offered in gratitude. We were all safe and there was absolutely nothing that was more important than that.

It took us hours and hours of digging to free the wagon. Periodically we'd bring some camels back into harness and see if we'd freed it enough for them to pull it out, always holding my breath in the desperate hope that we had, but it took several attempts before the wagon lurched forward and we were finally free. My body had never worked so hard. I hadn't even known I had arm muscles until we'd left on our trip, I'd certainly never used them.

Dusk was dancing all around us as we gave the camels the command to 'pull em up' and watched the wagon lurch forward, back onto the track. It had taken so much effort to un-bog our wagon, we'd even had to clear fallen branches that prevented us moving forward. As the daylight had faded I had begun to think we would have to camp bogged in the sand and I felt so relieved when the wagon moved that we hadn't needed to do that. I never liked waking up to yesterday's problem on a fresh new day.

Like many previous nights, we were so close to our camp from the night before that we could have used the same fire pit without too much inconvenience but nursing our wounds, our battered and bruised egos and dreaming of cigarettes that we didn't have and were unlikely to get, we dug a fresh pit for the fire and put the billy on to boil. When all else fails, make a cup of tea!

It had been a long time since we'd been smokers, but I was yearning for them, craving them like never before, obsessively wondering if a car would pass and if they would have some, and praying that they would. I'd given them up a long time ago but now their scrawny illusion of joy consumed me. Forget all this stress, I wanted to puff my way along hairy knife edged ridges with not a care in the world. I wanted to chain smoke through my next encounter with a bull camel and the next time we rolled the wagon down a treacherous hill, I'd sit with Zu watching from the safety of a shady tree puffing away until the last vestige of danger had passed.

Gill passed me a cup of tea and with his usual wry humor that often managed to put a laugh into what felt quite dire, made some quip about how he always knew how to show me a good time. We could have both been up to our necks in quick sand, just about to be sucked under and Gill would have come up with some funny one liner like, "Race ya!" which would have at least taken us out of our doomed reality with a big smile on our faces.

It's always good to be able to laugh at yourself but sometimes it just took me a little longer to get there, and even though what we were doing pushed every single emotion, had me rocketing skyward with joy one minute and tumbling into gloom the next, we had both laughed more on this trip then we had done for years and had really laughed too. I knew, however much I raged about our battle, that some days which bore the facade of a military combat rather than the whimsical romance of a trip that had been dreamt into life over red wine, moonlight and an open fire, my passing moods could change and transform as quickly as they came. If I'd really been given the choice to return to what we'd had or carry on, there would have been no deliberation, no pause for thought. Even with my still bruised face and an ego that had shrunk to the size of a dried pea, I would have chosen every time to keep going because despite all my fluctuating moods, I'm an optimist. I really did believe we could succeed in harmoniously travelling with all these animals and I didn't think for one moment that the daily struggle our lives had become would last for long.

Oh yes, I had many times I doubted, but every time I did I'd remember standing in that holy circle with all our camels and feeling the grace and blessings of those eagles, or I'd feel the presence of Mother Mary. We had been guided so many times and felt a force that was way beyond little us and it had flushed us out of our little lives. It had made remaining as we were impossible. It had given us no other option but this journey. This mad, crazy impossible journey with all these animals and the sheer fucking volume of holy, was forcing us to grow. We had to grow beyond our own limitations a thousand times and then bust out even more beyond that. We had to become the people that believed we could walk on water because we would not succeed playing small.

And in those earlier days FUCK and holy could and often were experienced in the same laboured breath. As I cavorted between extremes of emotion, either being dragged along scratched and bloodied, or falling to my knees in utter awe and prayer at the indisputable magnificence of my life as I watched the silvery moon rise from the top of a deep red sand dune, I thought it was the animals that would get better, not me. I was still looking for the source of the problem outside myself and not within.

Sometimes we get things so utterly wrong and sometimes we are just blind but every experience offers us the chance to grow, if we are willing and I was. I definitely was!

Twenty-four

Run For Your Life

By the time I woke the following morning, Gill was already up lighting the fire. I'd slept so badly. The silence of the night had been disrupted by the throb of a generator from a small farm, just a couple of kilometres away that I knew we would pass by in a couple of days.

Gill wanted to stop for a day or two and work on the brakes. He was sure that with some adjustments they would work a lot better. I felt so relieved to hear that. While the noise of the night had certainly made sleep difficult, I'd also gone to bed worried. How could we continue if we couldn't stop or even slow our wagon down on a hill? The simple truth was we couldn't.

We were constantly stopping and starting for jobs we'd been unable to foresee because you can't do practice runs of real life and there were so many aspects of our trip, including with the wagon, that we had to stop and readjust. There had been no slight inclines we'd been able to do test runs down with a fully loaded wagon to check and see if the brakes did indeed work. No opportunities to travel down a bumpy corrugated road, with a wagon loaded with food and eight hundred litres of water so we could be certain Gill's self-taught welds held. Mostly they did. Only one had needed strengthening but it was comforting to know that if anything did need fixing, we had a welder.

It took Gill a few days to fix the brake and when we set off again, we both felt happy and confident knowing it was working. We'd both been confused about where the old Ghan line had gone. We were following a well-used track and could find no sign of where the old railway had run through. There wasn't even a dog spike. We couldn't understand where we had lost our way. Some of the properties we travelled through were hundreds of thousands of acres. You could travel a thousand kilometers in this country and not pass a station homestead, so it was fortuitous to know that just ahead was a small farm where we could at least ask for directions. All we had to do was follow the track to that throb. I was so over the din of that generator and couldn't wait to be out of its range. When we finally arrived, our track was blocked by the farm's gate. We were unprepared for this and Gill went in to meet the owner to find out where we'd lost the track we'd followed from Alice.

The farm was a 300 acre freehold property, right in the middle of station country. Jim, the owner, ran and worked it more or less by himself. He was a short and stocky, strong looking man with huge well worked hands which were covered in scars, bumps and crevices. We'd find out later that this man was so strong he was almost more useful than a tractor. He lived alone most of the time and was very welcoming of visitors. He invited us to fill our water tanks and made us a cuppa while they filled. We hadn't realised that the old Ghan Line finished at Jim's farm's gate and started again about 20 kilometres south. It was still in existence, but only the bare bones of a track that hadn't been used for the twenty years Jim had lived there. The property was one of the old railway sidings that he'd bought years ago when the railway closed down and because he had fenced that portion of it, the original route had been blocked.

It was getting late in the day and Jim was happy for us to camp on the edge of his drive for the night. We were keen to leave the next day and travel to the road that would take us south to where the old Ghan line recommenced. We'd had so many hold ups and I know life was continually showing me to stay present and let go to the flow, but if we didn't make some serious miles and soon, we would be travelling through the hottest part of the year. I was trying to let go and to trust in the flow but I felt stressed and it didn't help my mood that I had yet another hellish night of barely any sleep.

Jim's generator crashed through the stillness of the moonlit night, and when it finally stilled, it was only a small reprieve. At 4am it cranked into action again. When we rose the next day we were both knackered, though so very keen to go.

We followed a more direct track to the main road that would take us south and avoid us returning the way we'd come. Only a kilometre down the track, we came to a creek crossing. Gill had spent hours working on the brake and was very confident it was fixed, and that we'd have no more problems going down hills. I however, felt anxious. It had been terrifying being out in front, running for my life and not knowing if I was going to make it or be trampled to death. I didn't want to be a drama queen, but really, I could have died.

There I was once again, out in front leading the camels in my own replay of Groundhog Day. As I came over the brow of the hill and began to descend, I laughingly called back to Gill, "If that brake doesn't work, that's it. I mean it, I'm leaving!"

"Don't worry, it'll work fine," my love replied confidently and without a whisper of doubt. "I've fixed it."

It was still early in the morning and yet the heat of the sun had already leached the colour from the day, sucked all the blue from the sky, and I could feel myself breaking into a clammy sweat. As I took the first step that committed us all to moving downhill, I felt reassured that Zu was walking behind me. It had to be a good sign that he hadn't baled, perhaps because it wasn't as steep as the last hill and there was more room as the track was much wider. It wasn't until the wagon crested the brow and began its descent that the speed began to pick up. My stride became brisker and faster and then turned into a run. The camels were bounding along behind me. The wagon was barreling down the hill and I was once again screaming,

"Brake! Put the fucking brake on!" And thenI heard Gill's voice yelling from behind,"Run Kye, run!"

When I heard those words, I felt like bashing my beloved. I was so mad, I could have pulled him from the wagon by the scruff of his neck and knocked his precious Acubra hat off his head. That hat got so much attention. It was washed, shaped, primped, stitched and coddled like a pampered pet. I wanted to grind it savagely into the dirt with my dust covered work boots and blistered feet as I screamed and screamed and screamed.

But there was no time for that! I was running for my life and when we finally came to a halt, this time still on the track, I collapsed on the ground gasping for breath, too exhausted to even feel mad. I knew Gill would never willingly put me in danger. He was as shocked as I was, he'd felt certain he'd fixed the problem. He was always a beautiful protector and guardian of those he loves and seeing me running so fast and being unable to do anything to help me had scared the shit out of him.

I lay on my back in the dirt. It was hard to recall the woman I'd been, who'd worn beautiful clothes and loved getting dressed up. That life seemed like some far away dream. I had morphed into the opposite version of myself in every way. I'd left with such high ideals and not for one minute had I envisaged me laying in the dirt with such disregard for whether I'd dirty my clothes or attract the stares of a passing stranger. Nor had I ever imagined how I'd crawl on my hands and knees, sifting through the sand as I searched in manic desperation for a cigarette butt I knew I'd never find, in the middle of nowhere. I'd sunk so low and soared so high and yet I had *never* lived life so fully, though I did hope a time would come when I'd crash a little less.

The camels were all standing where the wagon had finally ground to a halt. They were chomping on their cuds, munching up each moment, calm and still. Zu's lead rope was trailing on the ground. It didn't matter, they all just stood patiently, aware that us little humans were working stuff out, knowing we'd get it all sorted eventually. They often had more faith in me than I had in myself and while deep down I knew we would get it together, in that moment I was full of doubt.

I could see Gill sitting pensively on the verge of the track, his face in shadow, sheltered from the sun by his hat. *How could I have ever thought I'd like to crush it.* I'd hurt it once and it hadn't felt good. Many months previously, in a rage, I'd cut the brim of his hat with some scissors. Not a huge cut, just enough to let him know I was mad. He'd looked so hurt when he first saw my almost clinical cut. I'd felt so mean, I couldn't do enough to make up to him. As I'd cooked his favorite meal, he had sat with a needle and thread carefully stitching up the cut with tight little black stitches. The memory of a wound that I could still see as I lay in the dirt watching him, feeling anxious in anticipation of what he would say. I knew he was thinking through his options, mulling them over. He always took his time, never one to throw ideas around. He always thought things through carefully, looking at ideas from every angle before he even muttered them to me. If Gill was a book, he was already edited - whereas I was the rough draught or the more raunchy version.

I swatted flies from my eyes, trying to rein in my impatience, waiting for him to speak and when he did, I was totally unprepared for what he had to say. He told me he wasn't prepared to take *any* more chances and he *had* to make a decision that would, without fail, guarantee we had working brakes. The hills we had encountered so far were only tiny sand hills and he knew we had some big ones coming up.

In the days of animal drawn wagons, the old roads would have meandered around the steep hills where ever possible, whereas with modern vehicles they went straight up and down and could be lethal if you were travelling in the old ways like us. Working brakes would mean the difference between life and death. I knew that whatever Gill had decided on, there was no negotiation from me - we *had* to get this right.

Gill knew I was not going to like his decision and it was the last thing he wanted to do, but the *only* solution he could think of was to replace the back axle with a much stronger one. He had a bigger heavy duty axle with a better hydraulic braking system in Alice Springs that needed some work done on it at the mechanics before he could fit it in our wagon. With the help of some friends, he reckoned he could have it all fixed and in place hopefully within the next week or two.

I blanched when he told me that. I could not have felt more frustrated at the prospect of being held up for an indefinite amount of time but there was nothing I could do. *Nothing, nothing, nothing!* We had to travel safely, we couldn't risk either our lives or the lives of our animals. I just *had* to get out of the way and let Gill focus on the job, though inside I felt like screaming.

Time was getting away from us and if we didn't get going soon we would miss our run with the cooler months and would be forced to pull up during the summer. It was already so damn hot. I couldn't believe that at a time it was essential for us to move on and get as far south as we could, we were being held up. I hated the bloody summers. It was one of the reasons I was leaving and if we didn't get going soon.... Oh, I prayed we would. *Please don't let me get stuck out in this insufferable heat without even a home to go to.* I felt such panic even thinking that could happen.

I buried my head in my hands. I felt waves of despair washing over me and yet I had a strange thought. I felt myself being pulled back to the past and wondering if any of the old Afghani cameleers that had also travelled this route had ever sat down by the side of the track feeling desperately weary and wept. Had they even done so on this very place where I sat, face in my hands feeling hopeless and in despair? I could almost hear the voices still echoing from a past time as they sat on their woven mats facing Mecca, faltering in their prayers as like me, they also cursed the wretched flies who gave no respite - flies that had trampled through dung and decay and now clustered thirstily in the corners of my teary eyes in their torturous onslaught to drink from the juices of my worn out body.

There was always something to struggle with in this harsh arid land. If it wasn't the frenzied attack of the flies, it was the rapacious brutes of burs that seemed ubiquitous with the Australian bush. They matted and pierced and got into everything and there was never a way to escape, no safe haven anywhere. The bogan fleas, tiny needle like prickles that got stuck in your jumper, tangled in your hair, matted in your bedding and when you sat on the ground pricked your flesh through the seat of your pants, or the three corned jacks with their sharp three pronged spines that stabbed the flesh so deeply they always gave a brutal shock. They'd had me in tears, sobbing desperately many a time.

Had those cameleers of old ever sat by their broken-down wagons like I did now and dreamt of the home of their birth? Our roots were different and the land they would have yearned for would have been harsher than mine, but softer than this arid wilderness that could break you with just its little toe and pulverise those quaint old dreams into dust.

Oh, to lie in grass that held no curse and feel safe under a soft warm sun, to be in a landscape that beckoned and didn't threaten, where the only plant to harm was the sting from the nettle. How this savage country mocked my own gentle Kentish roots. I didn't want to prolong this trip. For sure I wanted an adventure, but a couple of months would do me fine and then let me settle back down into domestic complacency in our dreamt of, trip survived, animals all safe, new home. I'm a homebody, not a gypsy or a traveller of rough seas. I'm like the trees, I need my roots to go deep down into the soil but in that moment, I knew there was no other choice but to pull up until the wagon was fixed and we could safely travel on. As I struggled to make peace with my impatience I had no idea that a series of events would unfold that would eventually lead me to a place of surrender. Only then would I get to face some hard truths. Truths I'd already glimpsed but never truly seen the full extent of.

I'd left on this trip with so much unnecessary baggage and it had never been the camels that needed training, it was me!

Twenty-five

Surrender

Why did I always fight everything? I should have known by now that everything flowed and was much easier when I let go. I was so damn stubborn and as I sat in camp, I felt frustrated with myself. After being endlessly busy for years, I'd unexpectedly come to a halt and yet my body was still in the momentum of being on the go. Gill had all these jobs he had to do. Speaking with friends and organizing someone with a trailer to pick up the axle that he'd left sitting in long grass at a friend's place, and ringing brake specialists to see if they could attach some brake drums to his axle. I felt at a loose end.

We parked our wagon under the shade of some gum trees on the edge of a dried out creek, a scene that was getting all too familiar as the outback is full of dried creeks that only run in the wet, and the biggest trees grow on these creek edges. As shelterers from the sun, the biggest trees were the most appealing for us to camp near. Often these dry creek beds were wide and shallow but this one was a small deep gully and wove like a snake through the bush. There was a huge stony looking hill that towered above us on the opposite side of the creek. It was covered in lots of small boulders, with stunted old bushes growing twisted from the winds. The flood water that ran from it would have been substantial and perhaps that was why this creek bed was so deep.

I decided to climb up the hill - perhaps looking down on everything would give me a new perspective. I certainly hoped so, and as I clambered over boulders and picked my way between prickly bushes that caught and tangled my hair as I tried to find the best route to the top, I had no idea that this was the first climb of many.

While this day I was climbing it to let off steam, I would also climb it numerous times, carrying my laptop in its briefcase, looking like I was headed to the office. A lone person in an arid wilderness, sitting atop a huge hill in the glaring sun on a laptop computer, because it was the only place I had the hope of picking up internet. Even then it took its time. It took me thirty minutes to even arrive in my email box and before I'd had a chance to open an email, my internet timed out. After spending hours on the phone in the preparation for our trip and explaining exactly where we were traveling, I had been reassured by a company that getting internet would not be a problem. They were very wrong.

I spent even more hours, dripping sweat, on our brick of a satellite phone while some generic assistant put me back on hold. However much I tried to explain, they didn't even appear to have the capacity to comprehend that I was in fact so unplugged from life as they knew it, and not sitting comfortably in an office chair with all the time in the world to listen to their mind numbing, continually on hold music. Neither my plight nor my pleas got me anywhere. I'd tramp down from that hill fuming and irate like I'd had a bad day at the office. It was all so incongruent with the life I was living. I gave up. I'd hoped to update people online as we travelled and that obviously wasn't going to happen, but by the time I reached this revelation, I was becoming more practiced in letting go. It obviously wasn't meant to be.

But the first time I climbed that hill, when every horizon was new, with every step I began to feel a calm return. The climbing took focus. I had to pick my way up a hill where there were no paths. Occasionally I would cross a small animal track made by the rock wallabies who lived amongst the boulders, but none of them wound to the top from the direction I was approaching.

I felt elated when I finally made it, puffing slightly from the exertions. Life below looked muffled and muted as if the tone of every little detail had been turned down. For a long time, I watched a silvery kestrel hovering in the sky, moving from place to place as it searched the ground for its prey. The air felt so thick, I even had a thought that if I launched myself from the top it would catch me and I could hover like the kestrel too. Could I hover so gracefully in my own life, surfing invisible currents and flows? From the top of that glorious hill, from that place where I could see in every direction and nothing stood taller than me, anything felt possible - even the idea that 'little Kye' with all her resistance and struggles to control could actually reach a place of surrender.

I cherished that idea as I began my downward clamber. Nothing in that moment appeared to matter anymore, and I'd certainly let go of my frustration of waiting for the brake to be fixed but I also felt cautious, humbled and belittled by all the past times I'd felt I'd reached that place of letting go only to fall flat on my face at the next hurdle. Is true surrender a place we ever truly reach, or is it just a deepening dive each time we meet an experience that doesn't look like what we want?

In the days to come I would discover it was always a deepening dive but in that moment, I had let go enough to feel determined to make the most of my time of stillness. Since the day we'd decided to leave on this trip it had been constant work and I'd had no time for myself. By the time I arrived back in camp, I felt excited. I was already mulling over the different coloured wools I had bought on the trip in the delusional notion I could crochet as we travelled. Every day had wrung me out so tightly, the idea of crocheting hadn't crossed my mind. Finally I had time, and while we waited for the brakes to be fixed, I had something exciting to do. I was going to crochet a jumper.

Our camp was only a few kilometres away from Jim's farm and on one of our visits to share a cuppa with our now new neighbour, we felt he may have the answer to our predicament with getting a regular water supply for all our animals. When we'd studied detailed maps of our route we found that many of the bores we needed to reach to fill up our water tanks were often several kilometres away from the track we were traveling down. In some cases up to twenty kilometers away, which meant by the time we'd filled up and got back to the track, we'd need to return to the tanks to fill up with water again. The weather was getting hot. We had certainly missed the winter run but we were sure we could still travel if we were prepared, and a plan was forming.

Jim had shown us a Toyota Landcruiser he was selling for a great price for a Swedish backpacker who'd already returned home. It caught both our attentions and I kept feeling we should buy it but we couldn't work out how we could carry water, travel with only the two of us and juggle a vehicle. Our camel team and the wagon needed us both to run safely and smoothly but we were sure there was a way because every time we thought of the Landcruiser, it literally purred at us.

Finally, Gill triumphed with the solution and I had to laugh. It was a 'there was an old lady who swallowed a fly, then swallowed a spider to catch the fly' type of solution.

Gill reckoned with a small motorbike and a trailer we could manage everything with ease. Each morning, Gill could get up and drive the trailer and 4WD ahead and park them at the best place he found for feed and our camp for that night. He could then ride back to us on the motorbike which would sit as we travelled on a ramp at the back of the wagon. This not only solved our water issue, it also ensured we always had the best feed for the animals. Even in the short distance we'd already travelled there had been several times when we'd pull up and camp at a place that had frugal feed, only to discover the next morning that if we'd only gone around the next bend we could have camped in abundance.

In some ways it all felt a little complicated and we didn't want to create any additional challenges through purchasing this 4WD. We gave it lots of thought, went on a few test runs through the dunes and both felt such a sense of peace when we thought about buying it we paid Jim the money, signed the paperwork and drove our new vehicle back to our wagon. It felt *really* good.

And there we were, on a remote dirt track, with barely anyone passing by except one guy from Alice driving a small tourist bus, who stopped to ask if his passengers could meet our camels. When Gill told the tour guide we'd be moving on as soon as we found a small motorbike bike to buy, lo and behold this tour guide had an ex postie bike for sale at a fantastic price in terrific condition. We were on a roll!

Gill drove to town the following day and bought the postie bike, bringing it back on an old trailer he'd scored for 50 bucks from the tip shop that he told me wouldn't take long for him to do up and register. And remarkably, I didn't even flinch at the prospect of yet another job and even more delays before we left!

Gill had already replaced the wagon's axle so it had a reliable breaking system and unprepared to take even the slightest risk that anything would go wrong he had built, from scrap metal, a second brake. This brake slammed down over the wheels and bought the entire wagon to an instant standstill, but it was only for emergencies. There would be no runaway wagons *ever* again.

I felt excited by how everything was coming together so easily. When you plan a huge adventure there are some aspects you just can't refine until you're doing it. I could see that traveling with our new set up would make life for us all so much easier and a huge weight lifted from me. We had nothing to prove. This wasn't some endurance test and our most important concern was keeping ourselves and all our animals happy, safe and well fed as we travelled.

We were only a few days away from setting off again when I walked down to move our tethered camels around and call the goats. I had a really uneasy feeling when the goats didn't appear. Even though I often couldn't see where they were grazing, they always came when I called but this time, the air felt empty of their presence and that made me panic.

I ran all over the place calling and calling, but there was no sign of them anywhere.

Twenty-six

Sacred Land

In the morning they still hadn't returned and I was feeling really worried. I was up at first light climbing the big hill, calling and calling out their names from the top, searching the landscape for the slightest movement and yet still there was no sign. Gill rode our new postie bike for hours looking and calling and didn't find them either.

It seemed like a logical step to check all the nearby bores and waterholes to see if they'd been there for a drink. We'd looked at detailed maps with Jim, and Gill found out the location of every possible place they may go to for water. Every day he got up early and went out on our postie bike in the hope he would find a sign they had passed that way - a track, some poo, perhaps some hair caught on a bush, but there nothing. Nothing at all, it was as if they had disappeared into thin air. He checked every accessible bore and water trough without finding the tiniest sign that they had been there. He even spoke with the landowner of the station we were on who told him he was mustering his cattle soon in a helicopter and he would look out for them, but nothing came of that. The only option we could see was left was to begin going further afield and searching even more remote watering holes.

To the east we could see these impressive ranges and Gill felt drawn to explore them first. Jim had heard that there was a waterhole in the hills but didn't know exactly where it was. The sun was only just rising when Gill set off on the bike, with his back pack of water and a tub of fly cream. The flies were giving us hell! I found it so hard to relax when he was away but one of us needed to stay with the animals. Gill felt he could cover more ground without me, but I was in torment not knowing. Had he found tracks? Was he on their trail? Would he return later in the day with them? I'd crane my ears, listening for the sound of the postie bike's return and when I finally heard it I'd run out to meet him, hopeful that this time he'd have the goats running along with him. All the time Gill was out looking I clung to hope, and it was devastating to see him returning each night without them.

Gill hadn't found any tracks. The ground was so hard and when it had become too rough for the postie bike, he'd parked it in the shade and continued on foot. He'd found himself following an ancient gorge that looked as if it had been untouched and left to be for years. Gill reckoned it was about three hours walking from the road to get to it and that's what had protected this sacred site from people and their rubbish, and all the way up this rocky dry gorge were rock carvings and cave paintings. At one place the whole side of the hill was covered with aboriginal nappings, the chips of stone that were left during stone tool making processes - evidence that in the past, a lot of people must have gathered there. He had spent all day looking for the water, even finding the water symbol carved into the rocks but the waterhole itself had evaded him, as had the goats. There was not a sign of them anywhere, but he hadn't given up hope. He was determined to return and find that waterhole and I knew he would.

He'd always had a really strong connection with aboriginal culture. I have seen him set off as if he was a sniffer dog sensing a trail, not knowing what it was or where it would lead. He would find paths through the bush that no one else would see they were so hidden, even climbing rocks he'd never climbed as if he knew exactly where he was going. Following these unseen trails, he would find little holes in the rocks with ceremonial painted stones in them, or other sacred objects. Sometimes he felt as if he should not have seen them because he felt they were women's business. He never touched anything, though once he went to reach for a stone and got bitten badly by bull ants - big, red, hopping ants about an inch long with an electric shock of a sting. These sacred places were guarded and always protected. You only got in if you were invited.

As we sat around the camp fire watching sparks shooting up into the darkness, filing the air with their tiny red embers like stars in a dark sky, we both felt low about the absence of our missing goats. I was certain though, Gill would find them soon. It was only a matter of time, but time I didn't think we had. Gill knew he was searching for our goats in sacred land and it had such powerful energy, it wouldn't let anyone in. *When that land feels comfortable with me Kye, it will guide me to that waterhole.*

While I was worried about my goats, I could also feel the magnetic energy that was drawing Gill in to go and explore those hills. Gill was following a new trail and it felt to me as if he was participating in some sort of personal initiation. The land herself was beckoning him, watching him as he walked through her gorges and climbed her rocky surfaces, sensing the nature of this man and if he was indeed worthy. I had no doubt she would not find fault and what had been hidden would soon be revealed.

Each morning Gill rose before the sun, packed up with supplies and headed off on the postie bike as far as he could, before walking and climbing the rest of the way.

On the third day he came across a large white stone as he walked through the gorge and carved into its surface was a large spiral. He knew then he was getting close to the water. He'd had to climb to find it, high up in that ancient rocky range where the rule of law was nature and it had been a very long time since anyone had been found worthy to enter.

It was small pool of water in the granite rock, surrounded by boulders and only accessible on one side where there was a grassy shore. After searching around for signs of our goats and not finding any, he'd gone to the water's edge. He told me later he was so aware of walking gently and leaving this waterhole as undisturbed as he could. Even though it was really hot and he was sweating profusely and the idea of jumping into that cool pool of water was so enticing, Gill respectfully had only softly splashed his face before retreating to the shade to rest, before the long hike home. It was from his shady vantage point he witnessed the guardian of the waterhole. A creature so old and ancient, him and his ancestors had lived in these sacred places since prehistoric times.

It was a huge goanna that was about six feet long and as he approached the water, he began scratching and rubbing his flaking skin up and down against the rocks before going down to the water's edge for a drink. Gill had no doubt this wise elder knew he was there and had allowed himself to be seen. No-one made it to this waterhole unless they were invited.

Gill had sat in the shadows until this giant goanna had toddled off and before he began his descent down through the granite gorge, he left an apple as an offering on the shore. Hopefully this goanna would get it when he next came for a drink.

After exhausting all avenues of finding the goats to the east but replenishing his nourishment of the sacred, Gill began exploring the hills to the west where we'd heard there was another waterhole.

Once again, this one proved elusive and it took Gill several long days of honing in on where he'd been told it was before he found it, and after extensively searching the area he had to conclude there was no sign of our goats, however he did uncover a somewhat sinister tale.

In a remote area in the hills he'd come across the remains of a very old firepit and laying nearby, an old metal water container that would have fitted across the saddle of a horse, even a camel. It was well made and would have still held water, only it had been hacked at with an axe and there was a jagged hole in the bottom. Now water containers are more precious than gold. In this harsh country destroying someone's means of carrying water equated to murder. No one could survive in extreme heat without their water.

This whole country was rife with tales of the abuses perpetrated to the Afghani cameleers who often faced the same vile persecution as the aboriginals. We'd already heard a tragic and heartbreaking story of an Afghani cameleer who was shot dead as he bathed in a river, because the white men didn't think he should be polluting their water.

Intrigued by the water container and its story, Gill used an old tracking technique of walking round and round in a spiral from the firepit out, covering the entire site, looking for more clues as to what had unfolded here. Further out and hidden behind some rocks Gill uncovered a second water container and this one was undamaged. Someone had managed to get a container out of the way and stash it safely for later, but they hadn't come back for it. Why?

Once again, Gill returned home in the last rays of light after a day searching for the goats and following the trail of this very old and murderous story. There was no hopeful news about the goats but he did bring the water containers back and we'd sat staring at them for a long time. There was an energy that came from them both that was palpable and I felt an ache in my heart for what had been and my tears fell. A hateful crime that had been committed decades and decades ago and yet the evidence was still there, whispering its brutal story and Gill had found it.

I felt really depressed that we'd lost the goats. During the day I lived in hope they'd turn up and each night I crashed. Weeks passed and we still hadn't seen a single sign that they even existed, yet I remained adamant I wasn't leaving without my goats. Gill wanted to at least move our camp a few kilometers down the road to a lush patch of victoria acacia so the camels could have plenty of fresh feed. Even though I yearned to move and ached for some peace away from the almost constant throb of Jim's generator, I was reluctant. What if our goats came back to find us gone? There I was, resisting the flow once again so I did what I knew would help me see more clearly, I climbed my hill.

It was already late in the day by the time I made it to the top. I knew my descent would be in the darkness but I had made the trip up and down so often, I felt sure I would remember the route. If I did forget, Gill was below building up the camp fire, patient and willing to allow me to go through my processes so we all could all finally move in a direction that made sense. He knew I'd get there. I loved knowing that if I did lose my way, it would be the fire that Gill was tending that would guide my way home.

On a previous visit to what had become *my* hill, I had found a little hip hole in the dirt, in the shade of a scrubby little bush right up near the top. It had been scraped out by a rock wallaby I always hoped I'd meet, but never had. It was Gill who explained to me later that not only did these hollows soften the earth's hard surface, they created the perfect shape for a wallaby or kangaroo's hips to sit comfortably within. Out on the plains, these hollows also help in times of drought because when it does rain, they puddle the water so it doesn't drain away so fast. The idea of a wallaby's comfort being so intricately connected to the well-being of the desert felt so perfect to me.

When I'd first seen that hip hole I'd had an immediate reaction to curl up in a foetal position within it and that is what I often did. It had become my little hip hole too, my haven and my balm. When everything got too much, when I felt overwhelmed by our lost goats and needed a place to cry, when I was struggling to let go, ten minutes laying in my little hollow, close to the earth, was so restorative I always returned to camp feeling deeply peaceful and renewed and that's how I felt as I headed home again. I'd laid in my hip hole, sobbing into the earth, trying to find some tiny grain of peace to cling to over what had happened to my goats and while that pain hadn't gone away, I did at least feel better. I knew we had to move.

I had just begun my descent into the burnt umbers of the dusk, heading for our camp fire that flickered brightly in the darkness below, when I felt to stop and rest on a rock. It happened so naturally I hadn't even given it any conscious thought. As I rested in the stillness I felt what I can only describe as being lovingly held in the hands of something holy and so deeply loving, I had never felt more looked after. Then I heard these words. They spoke to me so clearly, they chimed truth.

Trust in everything that is happening Kye, however it appears. Trust in what you see as good and what you see as bad. When your journey begins again, everything will be as it should be.

Twenty-seven

A Billy Goat Called Banjo

We often called in and had a cuppa with Jim. We'd even taken him and a backpacker that was doing some volunteer work on his farm, out for a ride in the small wagon. We had made a really lovely connection with him and while we were not moving far away, we probably wouldn't get to sit with him at night again and have a glass of his homemade beer, so he invited us over for dinner before we moved.

We parked our Landcruiser outside his gate and began to walk down his driveway. I was completely unprepared for what we were about to see. All the way, were the bloodied bodies of shot parrots. By the time we'd reached his house I was *really* upset. I didn't even want to stay and have dinner. I couldn't handle being around all that killing.

Jim had been very apologetic and I think he was probably cursing himself that he hadn't removed the bodies of the birds. For him this was survival. He'd created this oasis in the desert, this lush 300 acre property and every critter from far and wide had moved in and was eating his harvest. Jim was under no illusions as to how I'd felt seeing all these beautiful parrots dead. I had been teary and upset and unwilling to stay, but I had not been rude and a part of me had understood. It must be so hard trying to grow crops in the middle of a desert when your lush green harvest has the appeal of the Garden of Eden. I also knew that these birds could decimate an entire crop, they don't just nibble around the edges and leave some for others to share. They often have the ferocity of a plague of locusts. And I didn't have any answers. I got it, I just didn't want to be around it, so I politely left.

I hadn't liked what he'd done at all, but I don't ever think this gives me a right to attack someone. I am also deeply aware that compassion and kindness only grow where they are planted, and anger and judgement only create more of the same. You harvest what you sow.

I'd realised pretty soon on in getting to know Jim that his relationship with animals was very different to ours, but he'd always been friendly and welcoming. While I did find some of his attitudes a little gruff and unkind, I focused on where we could meet and often that was our humour. We may not ever be bosom buddies but I wasn't going to condemn him over *his* relationship with life. None of us can live so disconnected to nature that we turn against it to survive, but we each have to discover this ourselves. If we are hating one another for our ignorance instead of at least being kind, we are emanating the very same frequency that killed those birds.

I had no idea as I walked crying to our car that within a week we would see a tiny seed of compassion had indeed sprouted.

We'd been down at our new camping abode for about a week when I got a call on our satellite phone from Jim. He had something he wanted us to see and asked us if we could call in. I had no idea what it was, he was very secretive over the phone. We *had* to come and see for ourselves! I had realised his farm could be a bit of a war zone and while I had no doubt he'd felt contrite about us witnessing his massacre and would be doing everything he could to avoid us seeing that again, I did brace myself in anticipation of what was to come. However, the moment I saw what he'd done, every bit of amour fell away from me. I could have kissed the man and probably would have if he hadn't been so covered in grease and grime.

Sitting on an outside table was a really ornate cage that Jim had only *just* finished building. He'd created a good sized birdcage and had thought of every little detail. Sweet little hinges on the door, a handmade latch that kept the door closed, a water bowl and inside this work of art, feeding from a bunch of Jim's precious dates was an injured rainbow lorikeet parrot. Jim had found it unable to fly and thought it had injured a wing.

After the incident with all the dead parrots I was blown away by this man. He could be really gruff and appear unfeeling but he was obviously a lot more sensitive than I'd thought. It would appear that me being upset *had* impacted him and perhaps this act of compassion was his way of trying to make amends. I don't know, but my heart went out to him.

He knew we'd know what to do with this injured bird who only needed to rest its wing and was released a few weeks later by us, in a much safer and more parrot friendly location.

At around this time I began to get a sense that there was an animal in need who would join us on our journey. This was new to me. It had never even occurred to me that even more animals would join us along the way. I didn't know what animal it was or where it was even located. I can only explain it as a knowing at the outer edges of my perception. If I focused too intently on this knowing, I couldn't see it. It was like a little cloud of possibility drifting on the very edges of my awareness. I had a sense that I didn't need to know and that life would guide the animal to us, and that's exactly what happened.

We serendipitously bumped into some people we knew from Alice who worked at an aboriginal community twenty kilometers further down the road from where we were camped. It was the same community the members of the traveling lovefest were from and one we expected to be passing through when we began our journey again. During our conversation, they told us about a billy goat that lived there who was getting a really hard time from all the dogs. They felt his life was in danger. Just as they said that, I felt a rush of energy flow through me. I knew without any doubt that this was the animal that was coming to us, but I had no idea that such an extraordinary treasure trail would lead us to him.

Gill and I were spending most of our days driving down long dirt tracks looking for our goats and one morning, I woke to a message on our satellite phone from the camel man we'd purchased Nev and Lady Caroline from. It said that our goats had been seen at his community, about sixty kilometers away. Could they really have travelled this far? We were both incredulous. For weeks we'd been searching a relatively small area and now it appeared they'd already been long gone. This was the first bit of news we'd had about the goats and I was elated they had been seen and I was desperate to hear more, but every time we phoned we got no answer. The call went straight to an answering machine. After several attempts to find out more we eventually jumped in our 4WD and drove down endless sandy corrugated bumpy roads to the community. We were a little concerned that we hadn't got the relevant permits to enter, but hopeful if someone stopped us we could explain.

Later in the day when we finally caught up with our camel man, I was devastated to hear that no-one had actually seen our goats, but someone *had* heard a bell. One bell in the bush! That was it. It could have even been the sound of a bird! I had been so excited at the prospect of being reunited with our goats. The whole bumpy ride there I had imagined seeing them when we arrived and all the worry and stress I'd been struggling to handle since they'd gone just drained away. They'd all be home soon and I couldn't wait.

I crash landed badly. If it had been a goat bell, all our goats wore them and in many ways, knowing that only one bell had been heard was even more devastating for me. The thought that they'd somehow become separated filled me with anguish.

I was struggling to hold back my tears as we got in our car with Lee and he guided us to the place the bell had been heard. We called and called and walked around and climbed a hill and called from there, but couldn't find a single trace of our goats. I was absolutely downcast.

We had just dropped Lee back at the community and were about to leave when I noticed a really magnificent black, tan and white billy goat who was tethered to a tree. As I approached this goat to say hello I was warned emphatically by Lee *not* to go *anywhere* near him. He was *really* dangerous and was going to be shot. We were then told he'd been picked up from the aboriginal community just down the road from our camp site.

I could only shake my head in astonishment at all the synchronicities that had led to this moment of arriving in the nick of time to save this animals life. This was the animal I'd intuitively felt was coming to us, but Gill and I had assumed he would join us when we travelled through the community. We had no idea he'd already been moved.

Of course we offered him a home, which created a lot of perplexity as to why we would even want such a dangerous and unpredictable animal. I certainly had a huge moment of apprehension and self-doubt when I heard he had an extensive record of grievous bodily harm. He came with a warning that he could seriously hurt kids and kill dogs, and Lee's advice to "Never ever ever *ever, whatever you do,* turn your backs on him and *always* carry a stout stick. *You got that?!*"

Were we being ridiculous? We didn't even have anywhere to live and we were offering to take in an aggressive beast. Gill and I both looked at each other questionably. *Have we both gone mad?* As two people who were already living rather a crazy life I am not sure if we were at all equipped to answer that question. What I did know and couldn't ignore was that I knew this animal was meant to come with us. All we could do was trust in that process, especially as we'd arrived just in time to save his life. Trust we would, but my goodness, welcoming this huge horned beast certainly brought up my fears. The worried look on Lee's face hadn't helped at all!

"You don't want him coming after you, attacking you with those horns as your driving along," he said. So we trussed him up in the back of our land cruiser as if he was King Kong and even then, I didn't feel safe. His reputation had floored me. I sat sideways in the front of our 4WD never taking my eyes of him the entire way home. In my hand I clutched a stout stick so ferociously, my knuckles turned white from my grip. It was a bumpy and uncomfortable drive home sitting contorted in the front seat, never taking my eyes from the monster in the back, who strangely enough looked happy and excited to be on a new adventure. He was like a big smiling dog.

I felt so relieved when we finally reached our wagon. I was a hodgepodge of emotions - happy and heartbroken, trying to trust, yet quaking a little with fear. We decided to tether our apparently dangerous killer billy goat on the edge of our camp just while we all got used to each other. We obviously didn't want him killing our dogs, we had to maintain some sort of control. He had huge horns and looked so strong. The rumours had certainly built him up to be a violent thug and yet as I sat looking at him I had to admit, he didn't look dangerous. Even so I began our relationship interacting with him from a distance.

My lack of trust in what I had innately felt guided to welcome seems ridiculous now. Despite all the warnings we'd received about our new family member who we named Banjo, he appeared really mellow. He was totally unbothered by the dogs who I'd been terrified he'd at least try and attack, and he let Gill get really close and stroke him. He loved being stroked and began affectionately and rather happily rubbing his face up against Gill's jeans. He didn't look mean or menacing at all. How had so many people gotten this animals nature so incredibly wrong?

On the second day, Gill decided to let him off and he followed us around like a loveable though pungent pup, even walking with us through the sand dunes with all our dogs when we went to move our camels around. While we were making sure all our camels were happy, he entertained himself by munching on the acacias and then he trotted along behind us as we made our way home.

It was only later that we discovered Banjo had *had* to be aggressive to survive. The kids had played games with him and stoned him for a laugh, and the packs of hungry dogs had killed his mate and their little kid. If Banjo hadn't attacked everything that came towards him, they'd have killed him too.

I was so glad we'd trusted our feelings and welcomed him, even if it had been in a lot of fear. From the moment he arrived, he just fitted in. He looked so content, even when we had him on the rope. I almost heard him breathing a huge sigh of relief and muttering to himself, *finally here*. As I had been guided to him, had he also known we were coming? Had he even been the one to guide us to him? I didn't know, but it wouldn't have surprised me. Our animals were continually leading me beyond surprise as they helped me expand my awareness. It was slowly dawning on me that surprise was a garden fence, a boundary to the miraculous, and the more I opened up to the infinite and miraculous possibility of our existence on planet earth and lived fully with all its sentient life, the less likely I was to be surprised. The animals were leading me into a completely new reality and they had all come to play their part.

There was no doubt this noble beast had some pretty anti-social habits, like peeing all over his face and some days he had a right old pong, but he had an energy that was so wise and a presence about him that you could *only* respect. I could imagine all the trees bowing to him, and the winds gathering blossoms to garland his beard. Even the sun would part the clouds and shine on a cold day *just* for him. He was a force of nature, rather like Pan and I felt immense gratitude that it was *our* lives that had been blessed with him. I knew I had to trust in how everything on this trip was panning out. It had been devastating for me to not find the goats, but to have saved the life of such a phenomenal being as a result of them being lost was deeply comforting to me.

Twenty-eight
Love Among the Sand Dunes

I hadn't let go completely of looking for our goats and I remained optimistic that they'd eventually turn up, but we'd been going out every single day for months, driving for miles and miles looking for them and we were exhausted. We couldn't care for the animals we had if we were never home. We had to turn our focus to our temporary home amongst the acacia blossoms and red sand dunes and relax for a while.

I could tell Gill was relieved that I'd let go enough of searching for the goats to finally find some balance. I have no doubt he would have stopped driving out every day in the aimless search a while back if it hadn't been for me. He knew finding the goats was important to me and while I always felt supported by him there was always a point when Gill's wise council would take precedence. He had made his feelings clear that he felt it was time we stopped. Our energies were getting too scattered - we needed to focus on ourselves and the lives we *did* have. It's not that he didn't care, he just has a much more stoic and flowing experience of life. He didn't see our goats as lost, he thought they'd be having a really good time. Why wouldn't they be?

Even I breathed a sigh of relief to have some time of stillness. There was so much acacia around that the camels had plenty to eat and were happy. Happy camels meant happy us. We finally had time to rest and sleep. Since the moment we'd agreed to sell up and leave on this adventure, I couldn't remember going to sleep without feeling exhausted. It felt blissful to drift off to sleep, lulled by the sounds of the crows, the soft clucks around camp of our chickens, even the chipping sound of Gill carving a wooden spoon from a fallen branch. Life amongst the red sand dunes was so deeply soothing. Finally, with some time to ourselves, I managed to finish two crochet creations - a beautiful patchwork jumper and a fringed shawl of deep blues that I modelled against a back drop of deep red sand dunes, uploaded to eBay on my next shopping trip to town and within a few hours had sold both. I was so chuffed. It felt empowering to be so far from life as we'd known it, doing what we loved and selling our creations too.

I was feeling so restored from our time of being still in nature and one morning, as Gill was filling the coffee pot and making our morning cuppa, I laughingly told him I was glad I'd finally listened to him. "You always know what to do don't you, I should listen to you more," I said.

"As if that's gonna happen," he'd retorted and we'd both laughed. Experience told us that was highly unlikely. I remembered a night so long ago when we'd first met. He had led me through the forest to his tipi. The moon hadn't risen and it was so dark. When I'd told Gill I couldn't see anything, he'd replied, "Just follow me and you'll be ok."

Even as he spoke, I'd felt the pulse of those words. While he said them lightly and simply to guide me in that moment, for me they resonated with profound truth. There had been many times since, when faced with a dilemma, I'd hear those words echoing like a mantra from that time. I didn't always heed them. I had to find my own way and not just follow Gill and that usually meant dumping a whole lot of baggage before I could recognise the wisdom in what he was saying.

He'd come into my life barefoot, carrying everything he owned in a tiny green canvas bag. I'd scoffed at his lack of worldly attachments and the simplistic way he lived, and yet it was this man who helped me heal wounds that went so deep that until I met him, I had turned my back on *ever* loving again. He owned a bit more than a green canvas bag now and life had certainly bulged at the seams for him, but he was back out in nature and that's where he thrived.

And we were both thriving, finally having time to relax and enjoy living in the sand dunes in the midst of our big chaotic happy tribe. I loved the lot of them. Even smelly adorable Banjo, who was always a keen participant in our morning ritual of breakfast and coffee around the fire. He was a right little fire bug and I had no idea how he'd survived with no welcoming hearths or friendly people to hang out with. He loved hanging out with us. The species barrier, that illusion of separation that nicely categorized us all was nonexistent at our camp. In fact I wouldn't have been at all surprised if Banjo had poured himself a coffee, some mornings he looked like he wanted to.

That morning as we sat around the fire gently waking up to the day, Gill had ordered me to sit with my feet in a bucket of warm water he'd heated on the fire, while he made the coffee. I'd been so used to going barefoot when I lived in the tropics and you just couldn't do that in the desert. It had only taken me one little nip to pee behind a bush without my shoes on and I'd got them splintered with prickles. One tiny little quick nip because I was desperate for a pee. I had learnt that lesson well and wouldn't be doing that again. The prickles had been agonizing.

Gill moved his chair closer to mine and patted his lap for me to put one of my feet in it. He was so good with splinters but he never used a needle to get them out, preferring instead the very sharp tip of his pocket knife. It made me nervous seeing him coming at me with a knife, but it worked. He wasn't just good with splinters. He was an expert in dealing with bush wounds and if he had to stitch one up, he could. When you're far from help, that's good to know. He seemed to be able to deal with any emergency and was always so deeply earthed, he intuitively knew what to do. He also did great follow up care. Arriving with a bottle of tea tree oil, checking nothing had got infected, bandaging, replacing plasters. If any wound got septic, or if one of us got an infection, it was a good dose of ascorbic from Dr Gill. We travelled with it in kilos. Even if a camel got an infection, we had enough. We had come prepared.

Gill was always so nurturing towards me, checking I was warm, cutting my nails, anointing my cuts. One night as we sat on top of a sand dune and watched the moon rise, I had put my arm around him and told him how grateful I was that he was in my life. "You always look after me," I said.

"Well someone's got to," he replied and I'd laughingly answered, "I'm like your job, you came down here just to look after me didn't you." And while I know that I also bring qualities to our relationship, I can honestly say I have not been a low maintenance babe. But one of the qualities that has got us through conflict and challenge has been our humour. There are times we have needed to work things out between us, to let each other know how we feel and make some changes, but there have been many other times when all that was needed was a good belly laugh, when we were just taking life to seriously. Creating silly scenarios that we both feed into that make us laugh happens very naturally for us.

We played this game with some snotty neighbours in Alice who walked up our cul-de-sac each morning looking frosty and unfriendly, with their noses pointed snobbily in the air. Perhaps our camels were a come down for the neighbourhood, or perhaps they behaved like that with everyone. We had no idea, but we felt the vibe. One morning as we sat on our verandah, we saw them go past and we began to imagine that all the love from our place was wafting around them. "There is no going back for these two now," Gill would say. "Yup, next time we see them they will be carrying roses, she'll be wearing rainbow leggings and they will be putting flyers in all our letter boxes reminding us all about the power of love, AND, and..." Our silly imaginings rambled on until we were laughing so much that we did smile each morning as they walked past with their snotty noses in the air. It was only a matter of time. You couldn't pass our place every day without feeling the love.

And as we sat on that sand dune another scenario began to form. "I know what happened Gill," I said, "and I know why there is an age difference between us. Now you know how I am much more impulsive than you, well I reckon this is what happened. We were sitting up in the heavens looking down and I saw all the animals being mistreated and I was so mad, I thought *I am getting down there so I can help them* and I just dove in."

"And I," said Gill, "would have been trying to hold you back, hanging on to you by one leg while you kicked and struggled and finally broke free. You know I sat up there watching you thinking, *oh my god what has she done. Is she going to be alright? Should I go in? Does she need help? Oh my goodness what is she doing now, she is going to get herself in a right old mess. I'd better get down there.*" And while it was a silly scenario we created in fun, it kinda made sense. It certainly explained why Gill is nine years younger than me in mortal years. But whatever happened, we always knew our love was special. We knew that we had been brought together in the most phenomenal way because we had a big path to walk together, and you needed a love like ours to pull off a huge adventure into the unknown with all these animals. I knew I had to trust in that.

We had left with so many animals. Neither of us had ever anticipated taking on more as we travelled, and at that moment in time we had no idea that yet another animal was making his way into our lives. A rogue beast that we already knew. One we could never ever, ever, *ever* have imagined or anticipated in any scenario what so ever welcoming into our fold.

We were about to get the surprise of our lives and once again, despite all our fears and uncertainties, be called to trust in the power of our LOVE.

Twenty-nine

The Power of Love

I had never given up on our goats returning. We checked our old camp every day for signs, but we hadn't been out driving through the bush looking for them for quite a while. One morning we both knew we had to go out for a drive. I felt like we were being called. Could this be the day we were reunited with them? As I jumped in our 4WD I felt a surge of excitement at that thought that this could be the day we found them.

It felt really good to be exploring unknown territory again. We had become so contented in our life lived among the dunes, we had been enveloped in the domesticity of comfort zones and routines. It felt great to break free. We stopped at several water tanks along the way and slowly searched the ground around them for the slightest sign that our goats had been there. It was so disappointing, there was not a sign of them anywhere. As we walked back to the car I was having this inner conversation and it certainly helped lift my mood. *Stay in trust Kye, you felt to come out and look today, trust in that flow.*

We continued on our way. We were driving down a really remote and rough sandy track in amongst the sand dunes when we noticed a few camels and decided to stop and have a closer look. Some of the camels had nose pegs so we knew they were not wild, but we had no idea who they belonged to. I was feeling much more confident in my camel handling abilities and didn't feel any hesitation about approaching them to say hello. If anything I felt excited, however I would not have been so bold if I'd had an inkling as to who I was approaching.

As we got closer to them I heard Gill muttering, "Oh my god, no it can't be, hell it is. Kye it's Abdul. Be careful!"

I nearly buckled at the knees in fright when I heard Gill say that and I felt absolutely sick in my guts. This camel had traumatized me the day I'd helped Adi move him. I'd met him several times since and my impression of him had never changed. Adi didn't register any of his glaring flaws and thought he was a little angel and in some situations, he was. Abdul was often part of her belly dance routine and he was always perfectly behaved. Yet give him free rein in a paddock and throw in some innocent and unsuspecting victims and he was a terrifying stalker.

There is no doubt he'd grown up with very mixed messages, and no boundaries *at all*. Abdul was like many other orphaned camels, reared totally spoilt, allowed to do whatever they want until they grow so big and become a menace, they then get shot. Narrowly and somewhat miraculously, he'd avoided the latter.

When Adi moved away and was unable to take him with her we were asked if we'd give him a home but without *any* hesitation I'd said NO. This camel was dangerous, though I never felt that was his intention, and many times I'd heard of his pranks and couldn't help myself from smiling. He was more like a giant puppy that wanted to play and didn't know when to stop, and his huge size made him potentially life threatening. I felt so nervous when I saw him walking towards us. I couldn't believe I'd inadvertently put myself out on the flat with this camel again. While I was reminding myself to breathe and trying to look relaxed, in the moments before he reached us Gill and I were calculating the distance to the car and how long it would take to sprint there, whether or not there were suitable trees to climb (there were none), and if there was anything on the ground that resembled a stout stick. There wasn't.

It would have been crazy to run and it would have given Abdul an open invitation to chase us. We had no choice but to stand our ground and face him. It had been several years since we'd last seen him and as he approached us, we were surprised and cathartically relieved that he didn't appear to be his usual menacing self. Instead he was courteous and polite and I was questioning if it was indeed Abdul, but there was no doubt it was him.

We stood with him for a while, giving him a pat and saying hello and when we finally walked to the car, we were both smiling and happy. It had been wonderful seeing him all grown up and behaving himself. He was such renowned outback character, I could imagine 'Wanted - Dead or Alive' posters of his big, drooling mischievous face plastered to all the trees. He'd certainly lived a memorable life.

Now I have to say that apart from meeting Abdul, nothing else of significance happened that day. I felt a little let down as we returned to our camp. I had woken up with such a strong sense that we had to go out, and yet it had led to nothing.

The following day we drove to Alice to stock up on fresh food and we unexpectedly bumped into another camel owning friend. When we excitedly told him we'd seen Abdul, he replied, "Oh that troublemaker, he's going to be shot this week. He's been causing all sorts of trouble." It appeared that dear Abdul hadn't actually changed for the better, he'd just given us a good performance. For a moment, Gill and I dithered in uncertainty. We didn't want to see this boy shot but we also knew how problematic he could be. *But look how serendipitously our paths had woven together. Surely we should trust in that? And was Abdul the reason I'd felt to go out? Oh my goodness, it certainly looked like it.*

It didn't take us long to agree there was no way we'd let him be shot. I knew we had made the right choice, it felt so right. This was Abdul's last chance at life. We got the phone number of his current owner and Gill rang him immediately. I was trembling in case the deed had already been done and it was such a relief to hear Abdul was still alive. His owner was expecting someone with a gun to arrive at any moment to put him down. If we'd phoned an hour later, it would have been too late.

Our Landcruiser had already proven to be one of the best buys we'd ever made in our entire lives and the following morning, we hitched up the trailer and drove down to pick up our latest, saved in the nick of time, animal offender. Not only had Abdul chased and terrified family members on the property where he lived, he'd rolled on someone's newish car and crushed the bonnet. I wasn't happy hearing that and felt huge apprehension at our compassionate choice, but we'd gone too far to turn back. After years of refusing to take him, Abdul was *finally* coming home with us.

In all the time we'd been working with abused, orphaned and terrified camels the *only* camel we'd refused had been Abdul. I was an ardent animal lover. If I had the means and the room to look after them they could come, but I had *never ever* EVER imagined us welcoming Abdul into our fold and all the way home I was shaking my head in astonishment.

Our loveable rogue was so happy to come with us. He gave us goofy licks all over our faces as we put a rope around his neck and tethered him to the back of our trailer. Then he willingly walked the ten kilometers home as we drove at five kilometers an hour, checking on him all the way. Maybe the planets had all aligned, or perhaps Abdul had finally understood that this *really was* his last chance because from the very moment we opened our arms and welcomed him into our tribe, he behaved like a little angel. The Abdul I came to know was so adorable, I fell in love.

We'd settled into waiting for the brink of autumn before departing. To have left in the harsh heat would have been intolerable not just for us but for many of our animals, especially our chickens.

After months of searching I was having to face the harsh reality that my goats may not come back.

There was nothing to show they'd walked in any direction *at all* since wandering off. This was so odd. Had they been stolen? Or had they fallen into a black hole? I didn't know and of course I still clung to hope they'd return, but we were fast approaching a time when we would *have* to leave and I could no longer make the goats a reason *not* to move.

We couldn't stay camping on someone else's land forever. While the famer had been very understanding and even looked for our goats himself, we didn't want to stretch his hospitality. We were very conscious that we were on his land and filling up our water tanks from his bore and several times we had left some money at his house and at his bore pumps to contribute to fuel. We were both very aware of paying for everything that cost others money and for the same reason, we'd also made a financial contribution to Jim.

When I looked at the incredible adventures Gill had been on in search of the goats and at the faces of Banjo and Abdul, both of whom would have been dead if we hadn't come their way, I found some peace in the flow that had taken our goats away from us. Who knows, they could have found some secluded idyllic valley somewhere and said to each other, *stuff travelling, let's stay here.* It was only me that was imagining the worst, seeing them as lost instead of empowered. They couldn't do any harm, there were no wild goats around so they wouldn't breed up out of control as they did in other places, and hopefully they would just be living happy free lives munching contentedly away. Even so, until the very day we left we would continue the occasional driving foray through the sand dunes, exploring this phenomenal country and it was on our next 'let's go and search for the goats' trip out that we met a very interesting man.

Thirty

The Desert Alchemist

Once again we were in the middle of nowhere, with huge sand dunes on each side of the really rough and seldom used track we were driving along. There was little vegetation growing anywhere. The countryside was inhospitable and harsh and so when we came over a rise and saw a big bold sign saying 'fresh fruit and vegetables this way', we were astonished and then intrigued. Who on earth was managing to grow vegetables in this harsh and salty terrain? We *had* to go and find out.

It was a rough old block, a few abandoned cars in amongst the junk with a shed converted to a house. It was so tucked into the sand dunes that unless you'd seen the sign, you wouldn't know the place was there.

An old bloke with two fluffy white dogs yapping at his feet came out to greet us and with a big welcoming smile, told us his name was Ted. He had really white hair and a long silver beard and blues eyes that were piercing. It was a stinking hot day and he'd been sheltering inside but he offered to take us up to his vegetable garden so we could have a look and see what we wanted. He had lots of spinach, kale and lettuce he told us as we slowly walked over to a fenced area. He'd just done a big pick of the tomatoes and the radishes weren't quite ready. He was slightly stooped, as if he spent a lot of time on his knees and never had enough time upright to straighten up and when I saw all the work he'd put into his gardens and how much he was growing, I understood why.

This elderly man was growing prolific vegetables in sand and watering them with salty water and they looked vibrant and heathy. He was pretty proud of his achievement and really willing to share his method that he'd perfected over many years. Ted pointed out to us the long trenches with really steep smooth sides that he'd dug the length of his extensive veggie garden. All his seedlings were planted in the bottom of the trench. "Each time you water," he told us, "the salt leeches up the sides of the trench and the vegetables grow salt free."

After filling a box for us of fresh produce, he invited us inside for a coffee and after being out in the glare of the sun, inside his home was so dark that at first it was hard to see. We could have been deep within a cave. I'd noticed his nicotine stained fingers so it was no surprise to see overflowing ash trays everywhere, and when I went to drink the coffee he'd made us it tasted so strong and textured, I almost gagged. Gill told me later he'd seen Ted scooping copious amounts of coffee into a pot that was already half full and looked thick with dregs.

As we sat around his table that must have had about twenty unwashed, coffee stained mugs on it, Ted told us how he'd come to be living like a hermit in a place that was so remote.

It was hard to imagine that he'd once been a police officer, who'd decided to go undercover when his daughter died of a heroin overdose. He'd been fueled with a rage that became his mission - to take heroin off the streets. For years he'd lived a false identity, infiltrating the drug dealers and following the trail of the heroin until he was summoned to go and see his boss in his office and ordered to stop. He knew by this time that the trail he had followed led to the higher police echelons and beyond to certain MPs, and he knew his life was in danger. After several attempts on Ted's life he went into hiding, morphed into a wild looking hermit with nicotine stained green fingers and had ended up marrying an aboriginal woman who he told us was rarely home.

"This is a hard place for the aboriginals to be," he said. "Too many spirits hanging around, but they don't bother me." And pointing towards the sand dunes, Ted told us that we were on the site of an aboriginal massacre. "The whites had ridden in one day, coming in on horses over the dunes and they'd chased everyone down and killed them. Women and children too, whole families died that day. Their bones are still in those dunes and some of them you can still see."

There was an energy in the room that was palpable, as if all those innocent and beloved people who'd been murdered that day were standing alongside Ted and they didn't feel threatening or even scary. They'd come because in the telling of their story, more of their pain was being released. What was happening in that room felt holy. It was no surprise to hear from Ted that the aboriginals had initiated him and honoured him as the wise elder and guardian of this land. He had a strength that I had no doubt was aided by the ancestors that walked with him and I hoped his daughter was with them too.

I could have listened to this man stories for hours, but aware of the sun getting lower in the sky and our need to get home while it was still light, we gathered up our box of vegetables and said goodbye. He'd lost his daughter, his career, had his life turned upside down by corruption and yet from this darkness had discovered a new path and a new purpose. One where he was honoured as a guardian of sacred land and knowledge and where just like an alchemist, he'd transcended the limitations of growing plants in salty water, devising a system where they thrived. Knowledge that had the potential to transform people's lives in all the arid and salt water regions of the world and Ted was very excited by that.

It had been a sobering and yet inspirational visit with this phenomenal man and as we drove home we were both mulling over the conversation we'd had with him. When we reached the dirt road that led to our wee little track off to the left, we were totally unprepared for the comatose sprawl that was happening in our street.

Pulled up askew in the middle of the dirt road were a couple of cars with all their doors flung open and strewn around these vehicles were numerous bodies. My heart almost stopped in horror when I first saw them. It looked as if there'd been a terrible accident and people had died. It was only on the next look that I noticed one of these apparently inebriated men was actually attempting to light a fire in the middle of the road. He'd scraped together some kindling and dried leaves and was trying to ignite it with a cigarette lighter but he kept falling over. Finally, he managed to stay upright long enough to light it and his leafy pile began to billow smoke.

We'd stopped the car, unsure what to do and as we sat for a moment pondering the scene, one of the bodies began to stir and crawl drunkenly on his hands and knees towards us. Then using our car as a hoist to help him stand upright he put his hand through the window, waving it in Gill's face as he asked for ten dollars, then immediately thought better and changed it to twenty. Even in his inebriation he was still able to recognise a potential opportunity and go for the best deal and although all his effort had been wasted on us, I had to smile at that.

We eventually drove on home. Someone had managed to drag over some wood and their once smoky fire was burning brightly and hopefully would give enough light to warn any approaching cars of this unexpected street party. Thankfully this bush road was very quiet at night. If someone did come it would likely be other members of the aboriginal community these people were from that was ten more kilometres down the road. This was the same place that the car load of inebriated visitors who, driving their exhaustless car, had stopped to cuddle and kiss all our animals were from and the very same place that Banjo had been forced to fight for his life.

I felt so grateful that Gill and I were stubborn enough to walk against the flow when we knew something felt right. If we'd listened to what others had said about Banjo, we would *never* have given him a home. We would have missed out on getting to know one of the finest and most noble creatures I'd *ever* met. He'd settled in with us perfectly and from the moment he arrived had become part of our tribe.

For some reason, he'd taken a liking to Bella and Blossom who always hung out together and had begun to follow them everywhere. They were definitely not keen to be accompanied on their adventures by this huge stinky animal with his great big horns who'd trundle along behind them like a sweet little lamb. Several times they tried to sneak of for a feed without him and he hollered and got himself in such a panic, I prayed they'd become more accepting of him and with time, they did. I'm not sure if it was because they had a choice - more likely because Banjo was so persistent. He just kept following them everywhere. He *never* gave up.

For short we called them all 'The Beebs', as all their names began with B. *Have The Beebs come home yet? Did The Beebs get a drink of water?* And The Beebs all loved hanging around our camp. At night we'd sit around our fire and Blossom would be sitting beside us chomping on her cud while Bella and Banjo, who had very similar personalities and could both be really stubborn, would jostle each other to get as close to the flames as they could. Banjo always stood so close that he regularly singed the end of his beard and the end of it was always black and charred.

Every time we made dinner we had to check that The Beebs were not home. They were a cheeky little trio and it was wise to have them tethered before we began preparing food. One night I was in the process of making a curry while Gill was busy gathering wood for our campfire. I'd had a really good look around camp and unable to see them, had concluded it was safe to proceed with chopping up the vegetables. We had to be so careful, several times already we'd caught Banjo sneakily watching us from behind a tree, tucking himself back in if he thought we were looking his way. Perhaps this sneaking around was how he'd fed himself when he lived at the community, he was certainly very skilled at it and he'd watch patiently for one tiny moment of inattention. I was halfway through chopping up the pumpkin when I realized I hadn't got the garlic and went to the back of the wagon where our food was stored.

Banjo surfed that unguarded moment for all it was worth, running into camp so fast and scoffing the vegetables I'd already chopped that were sitting on the bread board. Cramming them into his mouth so his cheeks were bulging and even when he saw me running towards him, furiously waving my arms and yelling, he knew exactly how many more mouthfuls he could fit in before he needed to bolt.

These were the happy foibles of our life as we camped in amongst the dunes with our tribe, waiting out the intense heat of summer. Living with the animals was always entertaining and even if we didn't always see it at the time, we usually had a good laugh after.

Bathing was another precarious challenge. We'd indulged in the luxury of a small bath tub while we were stationary that sat just outside the wagon. It was a special treat and a very deserving one. To be able to soak in hot water and get really clean was heaven. I'd loved my beautiful bathroom in the home we'd sold but nothing beat the serenity of a bush bath, with a fire underneath it keeping the water warm, under a vast brilliant sky full of stars. But even this experience could be fraught with hazards. If the fire was too hot when we got into the bath we were likely to burn our bums and if the fire was not big enough, the water cooled too fast. It was a fine art, balancing the temperature so it was just right, but there was another hazard we'd not anticipated until it happened to Gill.

He was in the bath, all lathered up after shampooing his hair and was about to rinse out the suds when we both heard the sound of pounding feet. It was Kushy and Munki, our now rather large orphan camels who'd been out grazing and had come running back home for a drink. They barged straight over to the bath that we'd also used to water them from, and began slurping up Gill's water. Naked and with soap in his eyes, Gill was in no position to defend himself so I ran out and tried to help, but these two were thirsty. Gill had innocently thought if he let them have a little drink they would go away and leave him in peace.

They didn't. Instead, they drank his whole bath so quickly leaving barely a drop of water and Gill covered in suds. It was as hilarious as the time our parrot Juji had hung from Gill's bum biting him and though neither experiences had appeared to Gill as funny at the time, it never took him long. By the time I'd come to the rescue with some clean water to get the soap out of his eyes, he was starting to see how funny he looked sitting there all sudded up with no water!

We even had a resident crow with a very distinctive white feather on its back who seemed to think he could help himself to any food he wanted in our camp. As we were most likely camping under *his* tree, his attitude was somewhat understandable. We offered him morsels we thought he may eat but he always dropped them on the ground with feigned disgust. Nothing *we* ate was crow fodder, but he could be merciless in the way he pecked at our dogs and stole food from their plates. To keep the peace, we put out a small bowl for the crow at the same time we fed our dogs. I didn't want to create a dependency with any wild animal but he was so persistent, he gave us little choice. After each meal, 'White Feather' would fly up into the tree we camped under and chortle happily.

At night after the jobs were all done, we would often climb a nearby sand dune and lay in the warm sand on our backs, looking up at the bright blue orb of the moon, or dazzled by the intensity of the stars. There was nothing to intrude upon their brilliance, no false lights or tree lines, just pure unadulterated stars. If we were lucky, shooting stars would blaze across the sky, while the soft jangles of our camels bells as they moved amongst the acacia toned like some ancient call to prayer. These moments of rapture were so holy I often felt like a pilgrim returning home as we made our way back down the sand dune, slipping sideways when we lost our footing, always reassured of a soft landing, slipping and sliding back to the wagon, so charged up by the reverie stars were even glistening in our thoughts.

We both felt so grateful for this little haven that had been our home for the past few weeks and while I felt sad at the prospect of leaving our friend White

Feather, for the sake of the animals it was it was time to move again to fresher feed. We'd already chosen a new site about five more kilometers down the road, on the boundary of the next property, where the old Ghan line track that we had followed from Alice recommenced a further ten kilometres down the road.

I didn't feel ready to leave yet, but I knew our departure was fast approaching and this time nothing would hold us back, not even our long-lost goats.

Thirty-one

Hidden Blessings

Our new camp was the prettiest so far. We parked our wagon under a massive white ghost gum with its peeling papery bark and were happily settling in when White Feather arrived. We thought we'd seen him flying through the trees as we'd moved the wagon from our old camp, but couldn't be sure from a distance. Our new camp immediately felt like home when I heard him chortling away happily in the tree we all sheltered under.

I was blown away at how well I was handling the heat of summer without any air conditioning. I'd always struggled in Alice and yet living in our wagon without any home comforts, I was loving it. It certainly helped that our wagon was a shady haven with an insulated roof and canvas sides we could roll up so whenever there was a breeze, we got it.

It seemed so long ago, almost another incarnation that our lives had been a conveyor belt of constant demands. Remembering to pay a bill, order fabric, or phone up Sue and see if she could work. However hard we worked it was *never* enough and our lives had been exhausting.

For the first time in years I felt energized and alive and I loved living outside with all our animals. All the grime of modern life had been left behind when we sold our house. No more TV - we hadn't a clue what was happening in current affairs and I loved *never* hearing the news. Our joys now were simple moments that didn't cost anything and could have easily been missed if we'd clung to everything being perfect or hadn't been so willing to find the joy in the life we now found ourselves in.

Whenever we drove out to the tanks to fill up our 200 litre drums with water we'd always have a swim and float on our backs looking up at the vast blue skies, sometimes spotting the wedge tailed eagles surfing the currents way up above. Some tanks hadn't been cleaned out for ages and when we tried to stand on the bottom our feet would sink into green slime. This always freaked me out a bit. I had no idea what was living in the goo at the bottom of the tank and if I let my imagination get away, I'd find myself scrambling to get out as fast as I could which always had Gill in hysterics and made me laugh too.

Getting out was often a challenge, especially if the water level in the tank was low. I'd have to hoist myself up by my arms, grazing myself on the rough concrete surface. I didn't care about any of that though, I didn't even really care about the green slimy goo. I was sinking into a serenity I hadn't known since long before we'd bought our house and in this new space I no longer needed to race through this adventure and get it done. I was experiencing the value in all the little moments of each day and I was loving the blossoming experience of getting to know all our animals, especially our camels.

One morning Gill and I were leading our big red camel Alice to a fresh spot to feed and we'd all stopped abruptly at the same time. We could hear a distant rumbling and hadn't a clue what it was. The three of us had stood there looking at each other with puzzlement. *What could it be?* The noise was so loud, the earth was trembling and birds flapped frightened from the trees.

In that moment of shared consternation, all separation between us dissolved. We had noticed this happening more and more with all our animals but this experience was profound. We were three conscious beings undefined by limiting terms like 'camel' or 'person' and what was rather phenomenal was that we each recognised what the sound was at the very same moment in time and all looked at each other, eyes bulging in alarm before preparing to bolt.

Alice could fend for herself so we undid her rope so she could run back to the other camels, before sprinting back to our wagon to make sure all the small animals were safe. The winds whipped up around us, fierce and strong. Already the force of this wind was ripping branches from the trees but worst of all, our chickens were being blown around like tumbleweeds. It was an effort to keep moving against the wind and yet even with grit blowing in our eyes and the forces against us, we caught every one of our chickens and shut them safely in their home.

Rolling in like a tsunami wave was the dust storm from hell and it was about to hit us. We had no time to secure our camping chairs and cooking stuff that was already being blown up into the air. We quickly called all the dogs, threw them unceremoniously into the wagon, let down all the canvas sides and prepared to sit it out.

Our wagon could be kept warm when it was cold, sheltered us from the rain, was a cool retreat in the heat and yet even though we were far better off inside than out, so much dust blew in that the air inside our wagon was a dark gritty red. I had my eyes closed and my hand over my mouth so I didn't breathe in sand. It was stifling, but it passed as swiftly as it had come.

We climbed out from our wagon to find the red earth covered in fallen leaves and wind-swept blossoms with broken branches everywhere. Our belongings had been scattered with the wind, buckets caught in trees, our chairs thrown across camp and our blackened billy hanging in a bush, but all of our animals were safe. And that, I was coming to realise was *all* that mattered.

I had never thought I would find any blessings in losing our goats, but they were there. Our sojourn amongst the dunes was proving to be life changing. We had begun practicing yoga every morning before we began attending to our animals and I had never felt so good. In this new life I felt fit and strong and very calm, and all our animals responded to Gill and I in a much more harmonious way. Handling them all was so much easier and much less dangerous, though we'd still experienced some reservations from Jumuna. I understood why she hesitated to trust us. People had taken her away from her home in the desert and separated her from her family and tribe. I didn't want to push her in any way but I had really hoped for an opportunity to break through her barriers and it came in a very unexpected way.

One morning as we were attending to our camels we found Jumuna laying on the ground, barely conscious. She opened her eyes when I called her name but whatever was wrong it had well and truly knocked her and she was very weak. Gill and I went through all the obvious causes and both felt it was some sort of poisoning. Could it have been something she ate or had she been bitten by a snake?

We wouldn't know unless we called a vet but we both felt her condition was urgent and her survival depended on us acting immediately. If we waited for a vet to arrive, we'd be too late. We had to act promptly. We had set off very well prepared to treat our animals in sickness and after discussing all the options, we agreed to drench her with sulphur first and then give her an enema and flush her body out. Yes, we even had an enema kit!

Jumuna had laid there lifeless while I stroked and soothed her as I softly spoke words of love to my beautiful girl. I told her how much she meant to me, that I was sorry for all that had happened to her and that I would do everything I could to help her find her joy again. I even found myself softly chanting to her, rocking with the energy from side to side as I placed my hands on her body and held space for her healing.

We kept up enemas and sulphur drenches for two days, several times a day and on the third day she began to rouse. She wanted to get up but her legs were still weak. She even began to nibble a little of the food we'd gathered for her. I was deeply relieved. I had been so worried. Jumuna had always had a special place in my heart and it didn't occur to me until much later that this was the opportunity I'd asked for. I didn't know if she would revert back to her old defensive ways when her strength returned and so it was a huge relief when she was finally able to sit up to see a warmth in her eyes that had not been there before. I crouched down beside her so gently, unsure if my previous effusive affection would be shunned and what a priceless gift it was to feel her soft velvety nose gently nuzzling my hand. It was as if she was saying thank you. My little mousey eared love was showing *me* affection!

Jumuna's sickness had given us that dreamt of breakthrough. Finally, she knew she could trust us and she was safe to let us in. I felt so happy.

Just as Jumuna was wobbling back into life, we got up early one morning to find Blossom and Bella in camp, but no Banjo. This was unheard of. He loathed being parted from them and hollered if he even lost sight of them. I was so worried something had happened to him. Why else would he not have come home?

Gill thought he could have wandered off with the camels who'd been grazing in a little valley a five minute walk away from our camp, so we set off to check it out. Gill began circling out beyond where our camel tracks were and he soon picked up Banjo's tracks. It was very clear, he was alone. We excitedly set off in hot pursuit following Banjo's clear footprints in the sand. Some bushes must have been really tasty because his tracks did several leisurely circles around them and then took off back the way we'd just come, then looped over to the east, then more circling of more tasty bushes, then back we go the way we've just come, then round and round the bush we'd go again. He certainly wasn't taking a direct route anywhere and I was certain we'd see him at any moment sitting sheltering in the shade, but the day passed and despite followed his tracks all over the place, there was still no sign of him. I didn't want to give up and go home but the light was fading fast and we had all our other animals that needed us. We *had* to go back to camp, but I felt so glum. I couldn't bear to think of losing Banjo as well.

As we approached our wagon, I got the biggest surprise. Sitting peacefully chewing his cud, tethered to a tree, was Banjo! We had no idea how he'd magically manifested back at our camp until Gill noticed some recent car tracks coming in and recognised them as Jim's, so we rang him to find out the story.

Jim told us he'd just returned from a shopping trip to Alice to find Banjo sitting peacefully outside his farm gate. He recognised Banjo immediately as ours and tried to lead him into the back of his truck so he could drive him home. Banjo, obviously a billy goat with high self esteem, had been adamant he did not want to ride in the back and had jumped up onto the front passenger seat and settled himself down for the trip. Once again, Jim had shown me his soft and beautiful side. This gruff man had let our beloved billy with his pissy yellowed beard and his gagging stink, ride ten kilometres with him in his front cab, home to us. I absolutely loved the man for that! and I was elated to have Banjo back.

Oh, if we could have put up a little picket fence around our sweet and lovely camp I would have done so in a heartbeat. I found deep red sandy earth and massive blue skies innately soothing and our camp was in some of the most magnificent landscape I'd ever seen.

We had all found such a harmonious routine together and all the animals were enjoying their new lives. I had been concerned about the parrots, especially Beautiful and Charlie. They'd been used to being in the biggest aviary that we'd built down one entire side of our house, but in the two years we'd had them we'd never really gotten to know them. They were a bonded pair of corellas who had been together at least twenty two years. I got the impression Beautiful was older than Charlie - she was definitely more timid, or had been until we left on our trip when she finally began to interact and play. They were loving all the attention they received from living in the midst of our animal filled life. They were part of our tribe and they felt that. Every single day was an adventure.

We often let Jo out and he'd hang out in a branch of the tree we camped under with White Feather, our landlord crow, but I was hesitant to let out our other two because Beautiful was so nervous and I was worried we'd loose her.

We'd also taken in another little galah called Yumyum. On one of our trips to town we'd met an old neighbour who told us hubby had given her an ultimatum. After months of being chased, bitten and harassed by this fiendish galah, either he left or the bird did. After being joined by Banjo and Abdul with their records of grievous bodily harm one tiny little bird with issues didn't appear to pose any major problem. We happily agreed he'd come with us and while we anticipated a few bites, we had no idea that Yumyum would have us in hysterics. He was the funniest little clown of a bird and loved to entertain.

We were so happy in our little bush camp and it came as a shock one afternoon to drive back after a days shopping in Alice and see that someone had driven their car in a big circle around our camp, even driving over the top of bushes and crushing them as they made fresh tracks through the pristine bush. It felt disrespectful, not just of us but of the nature and the land and I felt *really* uneasy. There was a palpable difference in the energy of our camp. Whoever had visited had left their ghoulies behind and it really disturbed the tranquility of our haven.

Everyone we had met in the area had been friendly and kind and we had no idea who'd done this, but we didn't have to wait long to find out.

Thirty-two

Love We Live

Early the following morning a ute pulled up right outside our wagon, crushing more of the vegetation so they could drive right up to us. A couple in their late fifties sat inside the ute. They had tired grey faces and emanated the beneficence of an overflowing ash tray. We didn't need to be an oracle to feel their hostility but we had no idea why they were focusing it on us. Even so, we approached them with a willingness to experience the best. We were feeling really good and whatever was wrong, we were happy to listen and help.

I gave them a bright hello but they sat in their ute, silent and vengeful, staring in horror at our wagon. The expressions on their faces would have been more suited to someone viewing mutilated bodies at a crime scene instead of a sweet little scene of a hand painted wagon, chickens scratching up the dirt around our camp, our doves sitting on their veranda and Kushy and Munki settled in the shade chewing their cud. When the woman finally spoke her words were choked and barely audible. "This was my grandfather's land and he would turn in his grave to see this."

Gill and I were both puzzled. To see what? These people had created more damage driving through the bush than we had and after we left, nothing would remain to say we'd ever been there. "I'm really sorry," I said, "but I am really confused by what's going on."

And I was. When we had given Abdul a home we'd been told by the guy we got him from that our camp was now on his family's land. Apparently there was a long, thin finger of land that was such a funny and impractical shape that it had never been fenced from the station. We had apologised profusely - we had no idea and asked if it was ok for us to stay there until the weather began to cool. He'd replied yes. What we didn't know was that his family members were fighting and these two in the ute were estranged family they never spoke to. I could understand why.

When I realised what was going, on I felt my wisest choice was to try and soothe the situation. I politely explained that we had made a genuine mistake. We apologised sincerely for that. We understood we had inadvertently moved onto their land and we had been wrong in thinking we had the correct permission. "We do need to get organised and ready to leave," I told them. "Would you be able to give us two weeks more? We will definitely be gone by then."

They both sat there staring straight ahead, smoking as if they were about to face the hangman and there was this long aggrieved silence before hubby muttered something I had to strain to hear. I wasn't expecting roses, but I didn't anticipate a threat. "Let's just say," he paused before slowly doling out his poison, "I don't like camels." His words hung in the air like an airborne disease and I felt sick and shaky at the thought of what he was suggesting. Would this mean-spirited man actually harm them? I didn't know, but I wasn't going to take any chances.

We needed two weeks to get ready again for the road. We'd accumulated so much extra stuff during our time of stillness and it all needed to go. We had provisions to buy, camel gear to reorganise and the wagon needed a couple of small repairs. I wove my words like an enchantress, completely aware of lacing the conversation with charm and spinning their sense of empowerment into everything I said. I was playing for time but I was also protecting the lives of our camels. At the end of my spiel I asked them really clearly, "So, can you give us two weeks from today? And we will give you an absolute guarantee that we will be gone by then."

It worked, I had disarmed them. I had no doubt these two had come to stir up a fight. Some people feed from negative emotions, but there would be no feeding from us. We were not playing that game. They gave us the best we could hope for, a sour grunt of agreement that we could have two weeks, before leaving.

I'd wisely refrained from telling them that there was *absolutely* no way we'd still be there in two weeks. I had never felt so motivated to move before in my entire life. I'd work day and night to be ready if it meant I could avoid meeting these two *ever* again.

We felt like we'd been dunked in dirty dish water by the time they left. Both of us needed to soap up and scrub away all their dirty residue. I had no doubt their behaviour wasn't even personal, it was how they lived their lives. But it took us a while to reclaim our good and clear space and by the time we did, we were laughing.

Our prophets of doom had given us the clearest message and there was not a single element of doubt - it was absolutely, without any hesitation or further delay, with not a second to dally or dawdle, time to get our wagon rolling and back onto that red dirt road to who knows where. Our time of relaxing in the sand dunes and dreaming of little white picket fences surrounding our happy haven were indisputably over.

We had so much to do. Life for us now had to be pared back to the basics. The entire contents of the wagon needed to come out and be reorganised so that everything we regularly used was accessible as we travelled. All our food bins needed to be gone through and a shopping list written of supplies we needed to restock.

We even came to the hard decision to leave our small wagon behind at Jim's until such time we could return to collect it. It sounded foolish to even say that. I had clung to my hope that the goats would eventually return and the prospect of leaving the small wagon behind, their little travelling carriage, forced me to finally face the harsh reality that they were gone. They were gone, they were gone, they were gone and they were most likely never coming back. We'd done everything within our power to find them and now it was time to leave. I couldn't stop crying when I thought of my goats and so many other emotions were coming up at the prospect of travelling again. I felt a rush of energy flow through me when I imagined setting off and I felt really excited, but I was shit scared too. We had a long way to travel and I desperately wanted to believe it would be more harmonious than our previous efforts.

Our time of rest had been so regenerative for us both but it had also dulled my trust in my own capacity to cope with and to transform challenge. Imagining challenges can be much worse than facing them. I know my fear of bull camels had burgeoned with my vivid imagination, but in the reality of dealing with these predacious boys we'd found our strength, our courage and our flow and I couldn't find any of those qualities as we prepared to leave.

It was also still pretty hot. If it had been left to us we may have delayed another couple of weeks, even a month. If it had been left to us we may have put up the picket fence and lived happily ever after, never to face the challenges of travelling in a camel wagon with a huge tribe of renegade beasties *ever* again, but it wasn't. The current that was leading us on was flowing with such a force that once again we could only let go and trust.

Our lives hummed with harmony now. We were no longer the wound up and frazzled people we'd been when we first set off. Our relationships with all our animals had transformed, and a strong and clear inner voice that spoke from a place of trust and not fear calmly reassured me that this time everything *would* flow. It was the same message I'd been given when I'd climbed my hill all those months ago.

A few days before our day of departure dawned I went for a walk, intending to find a peaceful place away from the bellows and guffaws of our camp and all its noisy animals, somewhere I could sit without interruption and meditate. We'd been so busy, I needed some quiet time just for me and when I found a big shady gum tree, I went and sat with my back up against her thick trunk and closed my eyes. It was a few grasped moments from the never ending list of jobs we had to do and as I sat under the boughs of that leafy palace, I felt all the tension and busyness drain away. Everything was flowing and that's all I needed to know. I had to laugh when I heard the chortles of White Feather, who'd just landed in a flap of wings on the branch above my head. If it wasn't my animals following me it was the wildlife. I would miss our cheeky crow but this was his home patch. We were his visitors and while he'd happily obliged himself of our services and joined the dogs canteen for dinner, I had no doubt he'd be fine after we left.

I looked up to find him peering at me really intently from the branch above, moving his head from side to side as if he was trying to work out exactly what I needed. Then he ruffled up all his feathers and gave himself a shake, and this little tiny feather from his breast begin to float down towards me from side to side, almost in slow motion and as I opened up my hand, it landed like a blessing in my open palm. It was his parting gift. A little feather from his heart and I knew he was telling me that there was nothing to fear and if I always stayed in my heart, I'd be OK. In fact, I'd be more than ok.

What my dear old friend was reminding me of was that the way forward was the path of our hearts. It would be the love we lived that would guide us now and everything would indeed flow.

Also by

Kye Crow

Ghosts & Ghoumas

Sacred Journey into the Animal Realms

Sacred Journey into the Animal Realms 55 wisdom Cards

Love we Live will be released in June 2022

Tracks of LOVE will be released in September 2022

Bones & Old Love will be released 2023

Dearest readers

I am a self published author and all profits from this book help us to continue to care for not only ourselves, but an already large family of previously rescued animals. The more books we sell, the more we can do to help even more animals and build our vision of kindness.

If you have enjoyed this book please let your friends know.

Share it on social media. Gift it to your friends. Leave feedback if you buy it on Amazon. Even if you didn't buy it on Amazon you can still leave a review there and this will help me build sales. And if you know anyone I can send this book to that can help me get this epic and beautiful journey of trust out there into the world in a much bigger way, beyond the realms of little me, let me know.

I am often so busy caring for animals, or trying to write my next book while bottle feeding an orphaned lamb, mucking out the horse poop, or welcoming the latest animal that's arrived worn down from abuse with their trust in people broken. Finding time to focus on building sales, attracting media, getting interviews, all of which would be an enormous help gets lost in the midst of all these animals.

If you can help, be part of our beautiful network - even if it's just by letting others know about my books.
We thank you
We appreciate you
and so much LOVE

Kye & Gill & all the animals.

About Kye

I grew up in the UK and I loved it. I never ever planned to leave. I felt so at home there. My feet always sunk deep into the earth as I walked ancient paths to holy stone circles on windswept moors, or followed the river to collect bundles of comfrey for my goats to eat, or wild gooseberries from the bushes that grew on the rivers banks, for a pie.

In my late twenties I came to Australia for a holiday. I fell in love and while it was a romance that didn't last, I stayed. For a few years, alternating between returning home, surviving a dysfunctional relationship that taught me to love myself and finally, meeting the love of my life, Gill. My barefoot, gentle bushman who opened up a world I had never known before of living so gently and in such harmony with nature, I felt soothed in a way I had never experienced before. Almost thirty years later we are still happily together. Our life has been full of crazy adventures and Australia has become my permanent home.

Australia gave me a freedom and it also brought me Gill and we have walked a path together, with so many animals in tow, that has been so deeply guided by spirit and so full of love I can only describe it as holy. We have lived simply on the earth for decades in the midst of a huge tribe of animals. Camels, horses, dogs, cats, parrots, chickens, emus, kangaroos and all sorts of wildlife and birds. They have all helped us
expand our awareness and connect in a much deeper way with the animal realms and nature.

If you would like to find out more about us, please visit our website

www.arkheart.love

and do join our mailing list for periodic love letters and updates on all my books.
Love Always
Kye

Acknowledgments

Writing this book has been almost hermetic, living remote just me, Gill and the animals with weeks, even months passing without even seeing a soul. My haven has been my bus, parked on the banks of a river under ancient gum trees that shaded me from the sun. It's been a holy time, a blessed time, and it could have been a lonely time if I hadn't had all my beautiful friends on social media cheering me on and helping us keep our sanctuary of animals fed by buying my books, Gill's creations and numerous bags of virtual feed so I could focus on finishing this book. Thank you all.
You are all treasured more than you perhaps know.

And thank you so much Andrea for editing this book and doing so with such love and sensitivity. I knew from the moment I sent you my manuscript, not only was my book in safe hands, it was in loving ones. That matters so much to me. I am so grateful.

If there are any mistakes, I take full responsibility. I could not help myself adding a sentence or two here and there!

Chapter one

An excerpt from 'Sacred Journey into the Animal Realms' by Kye Crow

The sun shines brightly in the clear blue sky, while a flock of white corellas screeches excitedly from the big gum trees that grow in the dry creek bed. If we are still enough, and squat down gently, we may just see the family of rabbits that watch us secretively from the shadowy depths of their burrows under the crouching corkwood tree. Even though word has gone out into the animal realms that we are gathering, open-hearted, willing to learn as we help anchor a new way of living on our planet that honours our animal friends, trust is something we must all earn.

Far off in the east we hear the calls of many eagles taking to the air from their perches on the cold, hard face of the mountain, soaring high into the sky. So high, they see everything! For a moment, their huge outstretched wings block out the sun and a shadow passes over us.

Come in trust, the eagles call. We are here to help you and we come with a gift. We will fly with you in your visions and guide you with our wisdom in your dreaming. Together we will soar in the heavens.
In a small cave on the steepest face of the mountainside a mother eagle fluffs up her feathers and crouches over her eggs guarding them protectively. Content not to soar she nurtures the new life that grows strong within the eggs. The birth of a pure white eagle has long been foretold, whispered from grandmother to mother to fledgling daughter. It will only be born when the people of the earth wake up to this truth: we are all intricately connected, all one, and what we do to the animals and birds, the reptiles and insects and fish, we do to ourselves. All the animals of desert and forest, of ocean and trees, even the ants cleaning up the carcass of a long dead kangaroo pause for a moment to look skyward. They all know that the time of the white eagle is almost upon us. Almost! Our attention is drawn to a herd of goats approaching us from the south. There is no hurry because with every step there is something wonderful to explore. You see, to walk towards their destination without relishing and savouring every sweet breath would not even

occur to them. A fragrant leaf to nibble. A mouthful of blossoms! A boisterous scratch up against a dead tree stump. A stretch and a play. They will get to us eventually. They are magnificent creatures with big spirally horns and wild and woolly coats and in their midst we are delighted to see three newborn kids frolicking along. Oh what a wonderful omen this is! It is significant that there are three. Life speaks to us in the wind, the stones, in each tiny grain of sand. Whispers of wisdom can be heard in the death throes of a rabbit caught in the talons of a hungry eagle as well as in the birth of these three baby goats. The same sad breath that cries of death gives the joyous cry of birth. Three pure white goats, three rays of light, the perfect balance between male, female and the sacred dance that happens in the space between. It is the union between mind, body and spirit when all become one and the doorway to the magical and miraculous opens.

Let us sit on the earth and soak up her energies, for the goats are drawing in around us. If we close our eyes and open our hearts they can communicate with us in their own unique way. It may be in words, in visions, in feelings, or an experience unique to you that you just know is from the goats. Their gift to us is their presence. In the moments when we frolic on the edge of our own precipice before taking our leap of faith—and those times will come—the goats, who are sure-footed in the steepest and most treacherous terrain, will be our guides. But we will face these challenges only when they appear. Why waste time thinking about what may come, when it is such a beautiful day? Time to have fun, and that's exactly what the goats are doing! They are playing on the river rocks in the dry creek bed, jumping from one to the other with a flamboyant leap and a kick. This is only a tiny show of what these agile goats can do; wait until our journey together climbs high up into the mountains, the familiar terrain of these precipice dancers. We will get to know them better then.

Can you hear the beat of the tribal drums, calling the animals from far and near? Its percussive beat, the same pulse as the heartbeat of our mother, is gathering her children from every realm. Animals, faery, dragons or fish, we are all connected, all one, and there are many animals and beings from other dimensions coming to share their wisdom and love with us, too.

It is almost night-time when the foxes arrive, creeping in from the west as stealthily as the fading day. With hair the colour of flames these beautiful creatures live in the potent cusps, where one force meets another—known in the sacred realms as the betwixt times. These powerful times of magic remain closed to us if we make adverse judgement of our brothers and sisters, birthed from the same sacred source as us, our kin, beloved fox. The red veined shadows of dusk, the forest's edge, the lap of the ocean on the shore, the equinoxes and solstices, the passing from life to death, even the faery realms that live in a hidden dimension, are all magical doorways that fox moves through with ease. One of the foxes comes forward to speak with us. Her coat has seen brighter days and we can tell by the grey in her muzzle, and the slow, slightly stooped way she walks, that she has seen many moons. She asks us to listen. This is the time of council between all species. So, understanding fox will help us gain awareness of ourselves.

She tells us she has a gift for us and she places on the earth a mirror and beckons us to look. What do we see? Do we wish to grow beyond limitation; do we choose to soar in truth? Now is the time to understand that the reflection we see when we look at fox is our own. Long ago, this wise vixen tells us, before people forgot and denied their very essence, before they stopped living in a sacred way and honouring all life, the animals knew this time of darkness and ignorance would fall upon the earth—and they were prepared. Each species had a role to play in the 'Remembering'. Some, like the camels and the elephants, kept the dragon lines clear and held the ancient earth wisdom; others, like the parrots and the hummingbirds, were here to remind us of joy. The crows and ravens held the sacred truths, whereas emus were our guides on our spirit journeys into our dreaming. Some of the roles the animals chose they knew would not be easy. They faced violent deaths and persecution because the peoples of our planet would blame the animals for what they were unable to face within themselves. Even so our noble foxes, and others like the cats and dingoes and wolves, willingly offered to come back as one of the mirror keepers—and none of the other animals envied that task!

It is people's imbalance and greed on the planet that create havoc and carnage in the animal realms, says our wise vixen. All we do is reflect the imbalance back. She pauses. We are all silent; we have felt her sorrow for her species as she speaks. No wonder the foxes hold back from us. They have been judged, condemned and sentenced to brutal and horrific deaths. Only the wise folk have seen who they truly are. She takes a deep breath and composes herself; there is little life left in her old and weary body, and she knows it. This night will be her last and as the day fades, in the magic of the cusp, she will take her last breath as a fox and return to sacred source. She has no resistance, no fear even. Death is but a cycle of life, not an end. To hold back the flow would be like trying to stop a healthy seed planted in the fertile earth of our mother from sprouting. She has given us the mirror, but she has one last thing to tell us. When the people of our sacred earth understand that the imbalance they see and judge, reflected in the animal realms, begins and flows from each one of us, only then will we have the key to transformation and only then will all beings be able to live in peace and harmony.